"Oh, how I cherish this book… like a perfect cup of tea on a rainy day, or the first bloom of my amaryllis, or an intimate conversation with a cherished friend. I keep it by my bedside. A gift to myself, a sweet offering to go to sleep with and inspiration to start my day. Heartsong awakens the inner songs of the heart, gently guiding the reader to look at the world through an illumined lens, to bless each moment with a kind of poetic artistry that comes from how we view the world and life, around and within us. He inspires a kind of intimacy that opens the heart and soul, gracing everything it meets…" ~ Marlie A.

"If you've followed L.R. Heartsong for any time at all, you already know that his writing is exquisite. Each and every time I read his work, I am transported to another place and time—to an intimate connection with Earth, plants, wind, sky, and also with myself. I have been treasuring this new book that I received about 2 weeks ago. I save it for quiet moments when I am able to curl up with a hot cup of tea and completely sink into a space of inspiration and connection with the deeper aspects of life, the unseen realms, and the voice of Mother Earth, all of which shine brightly through River's skillful writing. Breathtakingly beautiful, from the front cover to the last page." ~ Jocelyn M.

"There is no agenda to this book, it is not an instruction manual. Just a gentle reminder how much joy there can be in walking barefoot, lying on the earth listening to the wind in the trees, smelling deeply the scents of nature, feeling the connection to everything around us and to us. Of being creative, nourishing your soul & encouraging others to do the same by your example. To notice small joys and be grateful for them. An absolute delight of a book, so much gratitude to L.R. Heartsong, may you continue to walk in beauty, leading the way for others." ~ Anna M.

"What a gift! This poetic little gem will completely transport you not only into a slower rhythm of being, but truly into another exquisite dimension of existence. Reading it, I found myself sinking deeper into my body-soul as I meandered through the self-contained, bite-sized chapters, fully enchanted by the inner and outer landscapes filled with awe, sensuality, delight, and reverence. It's hard to say what the book is about; mostly the rich, sensuous imagery throughout seems to evoke a nearly somatic memory of another way of being, one in which we are intimately connected with the wonder of the natural world, food, others, and ultimately ourselves. For this bibliophile, to say that it rests on my nightstand is highest praise." ~ Marie M.

"A couple of weeks ago, L.R. Heartsong contacted me to let me know he was sending a copy of his new book, TO KNEEL AND KISS THE EARTH. He had used one of my earlier comments to him (about the Soul Artist Journal) in this book and wanted to thank me by graciously gifting me an autographed copy. I had written, 'Your writing – words chosen, scenes described, emotions created – touches me like nothing else. It is a beautiful gift that leaves me vacant and overflowing at the same time. Thank you is not enough for what you give.' I mean that now more than ever. This man has such a beautiful way of shaping his world and an even lovelier way of writing about it. His is a journey into profound spiritual awareness through keen observation, stillness, and intention. Since receiving the copy, my morning reading has become a sanctuary. I find myself returning to "Leaving my Shoes along the Trail" the very first thing before I can continue from where I left off the day before. The words of that chapter in particular, though they came from another, feel like my own. LR Heartsong, thank you for this beautiful book, thank you for your light, and thank you for reminding me of everything that's so easy to forget but that's so important to remember." ~ Cindy H. (via Facebook)

"I loved reading River's new collection of his Soul Artist Journal inspirations. He's a true healer. He's a dedicated soul artist. He's a delightful writer! Sometimes I pick up exactly the book that I need in that moment, and it happened to me with this book. The chapter "Shadows and Healing" gave me a perspective that I need to let filter through me. If only for that one chapter, it's worth buying the book! (The other chapters are truly delightful as well.) I look forward to the next one!" ~ Richard S.

"Thank you, River, for this inspiring and wonderful gift. I have read your words slowly, allowing them to ground me, make me laugh, and fill me with appreciation and gratitude for our beautiful Mother Earth. '*Nature always brings me home to myself – my most authentic, expansive, best self – the one who is soft, flexible, receptive and aware.*' Yes – most definitely yes. I urge others to read this dear book and embrace walking at the edges too." ~ Josie G.

"River, you are a gift! Thank you for your unique expression of spirit having a human experience. Your words craft the merging of the two, with spirit reveling in the awakened senses and weaving meaning from the daily walk-about. Kudos to you, brother!" ~ Jennifer Allen, award-winning author of *Bone Knowing*

Reader comments from the Soul Artist Journal

"I've been reading your archives. Weeks ago, I'd meant to begin reading – one or two every now and then, I'd thought, but rather I've found myself reading and re-reading everything I could find. You are an amazing creature. Of all the things we've piled up for 'someday', perhaps first on my own list is to speak to you at length about your writing and to encourage you to publish further. More widely. *Bravissimo*, you are..." ~ Marlena de Blasi, internationally bestselling author of *A Thousand Days in Venice* and *A Thousand Days in Tuscany*

"Your writing – words chosen, scenes described, emotions created – touches me like nothing else. It is a beautiful gift that leaves me vacant and overflowing at the same time. Thank you is not enough for what you give." ~ Cindy H.

"You have this gift of being able to fearlessly write absolute raw emotion. It is beautiful." ~ Susan Marie H.

"Every time I read your posts, I am taken. In. All the way. The trembling depth of your honesty and vulnerability. The courage to keep moving bare against earth, sky, along the page of your journey. The sacred masculinity is so poignant and needed in this world with the over load and over indulgence of the sacred feminine, I can only imagine someone will recognize that your work needs to be gifted to the world. Thank you for your tremendous perseverance, commitment and heart. You are a gem among men." ~ Leslie C.

"A reminder... that's what you are... a beautiful reminder. It's time to put down my 'stones' and dip my feet into the ocean. What a gift you've given yet again. Thank you!" ~ Gabrielle R.

"Always beautifully said. Thank you for sharing your lovely musings with us during the last four years! I look forward each and every week to your posting, as it always finds words that speak to me. I found you during your podcast time (I miss that BTW) and still play them when I need a bit of a 'return to nature' reminder. You are truly appreciated and I am ever grateful for your sharing!" ~ Susan H.

"Once again, you lift my soul to a higher place. Thank you and blessings!" ~ Shauna Z.

"Thank you for your beautiful words." ~ Barry S.

"I cried as I read this for it matches my world perfectly, and because tonight I feel the world's woes, and her pains as well as ours. Thank you for voicing it for me too. I'm an artist and see and draw, paint or create how I'm feeling but sometimes words escape me. I'm indebted to you. Blessings and love to you." ~ Lynne H.

"This is a beautiful bit of writing! I love your way with words. Such a gorgeous soul shines through with each one. Thank you for writing." ~ Joy P.

"I would like to say to you, dearest River... you are truly special. Thank you and thank you even more for this journey." ~ Gillian T.

"You are amazing." ~ Roger C.

"Loved, loved, LOVED this post! Thanks for putting into words... the art of food! You inspired me to go to my local city market this weekend, despite the heat predicted, where I hope to find a bit of magic and mindfulness. As always, thank you for sharing, it made my day... again." ~ SH

"Your words cause a stirring of the artistic... and a need to live more mindfully and creatively. Thank you so very much." ~ JWP

"As usual, this post resonated strongly with me and comes at the perfect time. Your writings always seem to be speaking directly to my soul, exactly what I need to hear... you so eloquently voice what is so very jumbled in my head. Your words never fail to move me. Thank you!" ~ Theresa R.

"As a late-comer to Soul Artist Journal, I have looked forward to receiving your posts. I so enjoy them, as a reminder to ponder the simple joys of life..." ~ Christine S.

"Thank you so much again for sharing your heart and reopening mine."
~ Pamela B.

"Beautiful, as always. Such a gift to read your words." ~ Randy L.

"Please... keep the words flowing so eloquently, so poetically and help more folks find their way back home to their deepest inner soul space..." ~ Mare C.

"This is a beautiful, vulnerable, perfect reminder. Thank you for writing and sharing this piece so sprawled out and open." ~ L.C.

Again, to the Soul of the World.

Once more, for all those who heed the call of their soul, contributing something of value and beauty to the Larger Story.

And for the Grandmother, a great and dear Monterey cypress who kept watch over me in my chrysalis at the edge of the world.

Also by L.R. Heartsong:

The Bones & Breath:
A Man's Guide to Eros, the Sacred Masculine, and the Wild Soul
[Nautilus Award winner]

To Kneel and Kiss the Earth: Inspiration from the Soul Artist
Journal

A Life for the Senses

Return to the Soul Artist Journal

L.R. Heartsong

Award–winning author of *The Bones & Breath:*
A Man's Guide to Eros, the Sacred Masculine, and the Wild Soul

Hearthside Press ❧ Bend, Oregon

Hearthside Press
PO Box 8507
Bend, Oregon 97708
hearthsidepress.com

Cover photo by @mjseka (Unsplash)
Cover and interior design by Katie Elizabeth Boyer Clark
(www.katielizabeth.com)
Author photo by Rae Huo

First edition: 2020
Printed in the USA

ISBN: 978-0-578-64829-3 (paperback)

Contents

ɜ ɜ ɜ

ॐ ॐ ॐ

Preface to the new volume

I'm not generally one for second helpings, be that of food, books, sequels, nor a shot of ayahuasca. That said, when I compiled and released *To Kneel and Kiss the Earth*, I strongly suspected there could be another such offering one day—if only because, having penned the Soul Artist Journal for nearly five years, more than two hundred posts are in the archives. Surely another two dozen or so were worth bringing back into the light for sharing once more in another collection. Eventually.

Admittedly, I was delighted when that first compilation met with such delight and praise from readers; a minor flood of emails and positive reviews, both from steadfast followers of the SAJ as well as people discovering those writings for a first time.

As written in the Preface for the previous offering, life rolls on. Evolution unfurls. In the years since closing the cover on the Journal, my life and work has taken me in what seems, on the surface at least, to be a very different direction—fusing vibrant health and soul. Yet *soulful nourishment* remains the ongoing theme, a golden thread woven continually through all that I do.

Dear reader, this is what has drawn me back to gather together a second selection of posts from the Soul Artist Journal: the hope of delivering more heart-full, soulful nourishment in an accessible, digestible format. Something easy to pick up with a cup of morning or afternoon tea, a few pages read, and just as easily set down upon finishing. (Unlike, say, the much lengthier and differently oriented posts of TendingSacred, the sequel to the SAJ, which ran the past three years.)

Once again, the pieces included here felt somehow *right*, if only perhaps because some aspect emphasized "a life for the senses," which was the tagline for the Journal. Also like the first volume, all the years are represented (you will notice a changing voice over time), but the posts are not in any chronological order.

As I so often say and write, one cannot fathom the Mystery. That my original e-column (I never cared for the word "blog") should live on, garnering continued interest and new readership, evokes gratitude in my heart for such a curious twist of fate.

Life continues to delight and amaze me, astounding with its sensory richness and serendipitous invitations—a sparrow alighting on the branch just beyond the window as I turn to gaze outside, the soft voice of the wind in the pines at night when I step outdoors with the dogs. I am ever reminded that, despite our seeming troubles, this human journey is truly a feast for the senses. A gift.

L.R. Heartsong

Early spring, 2020

Preface (from the previous volume)

In 2012, recently returned from years of living in Europe, in hopes of attracting a publisher for my completed book manuscript, I launched the Soul Artist Journal.

What began as merely a means to an end—establishing an author's platform to help promote my work—steadily shifted and drew me in. My e-column (I never cared for the word "blog") became a weekly discipline that changed me for the better, not simply because of what I offered to the world from my heart but the practice of writing itself.

The content, tone, and length of these posts evolved over time, and in a natural cycle of maturing the Journal finally found its authentic voice, "celebrating a life for the senses" (though I didn't actually adopt that as a tagline until much later).

> *"How easy it is to lose touch with the tactile goodness of our days, especially when beauty seems distant, or mostly ignored and forgotten in a harried rush. Yet beauty exists everywhere. Most of us are simply not paying attention. And in both the heart and senses, too many of us are closed like a fist, rather than a hand held open in giving.*
>
> *Daily, I am seduced by moments of ordinary, heart-fluttering beauty that I love to offer forward, just as I would something from my kitchen, passed to you on a simple, handmade plate.*
>
> *Be open, my friend." (SAJ, 2016)*

In 2015, I reluctantly ventured deeper into social media to leverage my newly published book, and spent six months writing weekly articles as a featured contributor for a couple of online publications (*elephant journal* and the Good Men Project), where I learned that shorter pieces are shared more widely and help build readership. Though I prefer longer-style narratives, gradually I trimmed the length of my own posts—for a weekly column, this certainly made life easier—and, sure enough, found them flying far and wide. Yet I wrestled with whether I was being true to my vision or somehow selling out (though certainly I will never be mainstream).

The SAJ seldom focused on the material in *The Bones & Breath: A Man's Guide to Eros, the Sacred Masculine and the Wild Soul*, partly because my role in the world is larger than "men's work" (valuable as I believe that to be). Truthfully, I wanted to reach a bigger audience, and there are multiple aspects to what I teach and share in life—that for more than two decades I have been a bodyworker, counselor, and healer, and I'm also a French-trained chef who employs Ayurvedic and healthy principles. Thus I cast the net wide and attracted both women and men as readers while reflecting on what it means to be a Soul Artist (a theme drawn from what I planned to be my follow-up book).

> *"... despite the occasional temptation to settle in comfortably and simply write about being in the kitchen, to exalt the rustic, local, seasonal fare that I love to prepare, I figure that the world doesn't need another food blogger—probably not even a French-trained, barefoot, nature-boy attuned to the subtle art of nourishing the soul." (SAJ, 2016)*

Those who read the Journal at all regularly discovered that I'm an old-fashioned, mostly quiet fellow who repeatedly encourages others to slow down and unplug from a wired existence, to take a deep breath and dilate their senses. Taste. See. Listen. Smell. *Feel.* I remind people (myself, included) to relish the pleasures of life with a heart steeped in gratitude, urging us all to savor the precious gifts of being fully human, even amid the challenges. Especially then.

> *"Life is not always art, but certainly there exists an art and soul to living—to cooking, writing, eating, walking and sitting, dancing, friendship, telling stories, making love—and it is a worthy goal to live gracefully, both in abundance and in need." (SAJ, 2016)*

In 2015, while visiting Paris en route to my beloved Provence, in a million-to-one chance, I met Marlena de Blasi, internationally best-selling author of *A Thousand Days in Venice* and *A Thousand Days in Tuscany*, while seated outdoors at Les Deux Magots, a famous café. An American chef who moved to Italy to marry a Venetian, and then later relocated to Tuscany followed by rustic Umbria, her lushly gilded memoirs inspired and comforted me when I too was an expat living abroad, finding solace in the kitchen or at the market. After our serendipitous meeting on the Left Bank, not only did we forge a long-distance friendship but also she dove into the archives of the Soul Artist Journal, and repeatedly wrote to me with accolades for these posts.

What a further delight and affirmation when Nigel Slater, Britain's foremost food writer (also a cookbook author and television personality) on Twitter praised one of my posts as "life enriching words..." I was, as the Brits say, 'chuffed to bits'.

Life rolls on. I felt the gentle tug of deeper currents and unseen hands urging my vessel down a different stream. In January 2017, four and a half years (more than two hundred and twenty-five posts) after beginning my weekly venture, I closed the cover on the Soul Artist Journal. It was time for a change, to turn my energies elsewhere—more precisely, to focus on the facet of work that most loudly called to me, which is the healer's journey, and to write from the heart and soul about that. Thus TendingSacred was born, a monthly dive into the longer narratives that I prefer.

Over the years, repeated requests have come from readers for some sort of compilation of the Journal—something other than simply the website with its archives. To that end, finally, a first collection of posts: some that I especially enjoyed or received a good share of attention, others because they somehow felt "right" to be included in this overview and time capsule. All years of the e-column are represented, though they are not chronological or in any particular order. Just as the weekly writings were diverse and covered a wide patch of sacred ground, subscribers never knowing exactly what topic might greet them upon opening the posts on Sunday (the usual distribution day), I have here chosen to continue that tradition; rather than simply choose a few categories upon which to focus (e.g. Conscious Living, Inspiration, Nature, Slow Food, The Sacred Masculine, Wild Soul, etc.) for the sake of making a more cohesive book, instead I have drawn from across the spectrum of what was offered. Regretfully, due to matters of printing cost, rights and permissions, etcetera, the photos that accompany the posts on the website have not been reproduced, and thus while the visual allure of the SAJ feels missing here, I can only trust that the energy inhabiting the original words shines through.

My deepest gratitude to all the readers of the Journal, particularly those who shared it with others, especially the dedicated subscribers and followers who opened the posts every Sunday morning with their cup of coffee or tea, and the generous souls who reached out to me with comments and praise. You kept me going, showing up at the page for five years, determined to offer another glimpse of beauty from the heart and soul.

Gentle reader, may you find daily inspiration to continue along the sometimes-arduous track in your own search to bring something of value to the 'more-than-human' world. And I hope you'll find a generous helping of soulful nourishment in these pages.

L.R. Heartsong
Autumn, 2018

Introduction: About the Journal
{From the SAJ website}

We all need inspiration on our journey. For nearly five years, the Soul Artist Journal explored weekly the art of living a meaningful, connected existence that cultivates a sense of well-being. Though the posts were diverse, there was an underlying theme: *how do we nourish the soul?*

What does it mean to be a Soul Artist? The SAJ articles offered reflections on those little, ordinary human moments of the day: a cup of tea, a fading flower in the garden, puttering in the kitchen, a stroll through the neighborhood or along a wild riverbank. Each entry, in differing ways, extolled the importance of opening our senses and heart to the living field of intelligence we are continually bathed in. How does the moment *feel*? What is on our plate to share? How can we nurture and befriend the body as ecstatic resource for a life of vitality and well-being? What is ours to bring to this multidimensional relationship—with place, humans, earth's denizens, and planet? What is the Deep Imagination? And how do we heal and *evolve*?

The Journal traveled its own spiral and arc, varying in length and tone over the years. Yet it always sought to illuminate conscious living and embodiment, gratitude, creativity, personal authenticity and transformation, seasonal food, natural beauty, and a sensual connection with nature and earth.

In short, these writings celebrate a life for the senses... and the ordinary sacred.

Perhaps pour yourself a cup of something, and then sit somewhere comfortable and quiet. Inhale a couple of deep breaths, sweeping aside the noisy voices and demands of the day—if only for now—and take a little journey for your soul.

Welcome, traveler.

❧ ❧ ❧

Author's Note

My years of living in England changed me, both in subtle and more definite ways; mostly for the better, I think. That said, I'm really not sure I can get through a day without proper teatime (and biscuits, thank you).

In written words, the lingering UK influence is evidenced by a preference for British spellings, though I generally keep to the American "z" instead of an "s" (e.g. "actualize" versus *actualise,* "civilization" rather than *civilisation,* etc.). Further, the Queen's English rules of grammar (spaces around en-dashes, for instance, and single apostrophe versus quotation marks) feel and look more 'right' to me than those set forth by that American gospel, The Chicago Manual of Style. And I am rather fond of qualifiers *(some, very, rather, too, much)* which the Brits adore and employ regularly in speaking and writing, but current American grammar regards as superfluous and cluttered.

Regularly, I notice my inconsistency of choice(s), switching back and forth, occasionally even within the same post, as if I'm a hybrid engine. At times I have thought to comb through past writings, tidying them up, assigning a passport and nationality once and for all. I tell myself that most of my readers are American, and if I ever landed a literary agent or New York publisher, an editor would certainly force the home rules.

In the end, I have not made changes, nor committed to either shore of the Atlantic. Truly, I'm not trying to be pretentious or affected. Even beyond writing, in matters of food, clothing, language, and general tastes, my style is an amalgam of Old World and new. And somehow this feels strangely right, reflecting who I am as a wandering, soulful nomad, gathering bits of what I like from here and there, discarding the rest.

So, onwards we go, and we shall *savour* the *flavour* of *favourites* with *colourful neighbours* and whatnot.

❧ ❧ ❧

Rewilding the Heart and Soul
(February, 2016)

I need to go find the deer, eat some wild weeds, and ramble beside a musical river.

While tree blossoms burst open in profusion all around, scenting the air with honeyed sweetness, and the earth is overrun by lanky, bright flowers of yellow woodsorrel, I've been gradually constricting. Like a lengthening shadow, domesticity slowly creeps up on me once more.

Mostly, I am content with the rituals of hearth and home; the very ones I have deliberately created in a quiet, handcrafted life. Yet because I live in town, albeit a small one, when I am too long contained by four walls and roof, by the geometric grid of streets, something in me withers. Nature boy that I am, I don't fare well when disconnected from my wild soul.

It seems like it should be enough for a soulful existence: greeting the morning with hands upon the grandmother Monterey cypress tree; a daily wordless communion with the beauty that surrounds nearly everywhere; hours of scribbling quietly by the window with an old fountain pen from Paris; the sessions with clients; a house free of television and radio. Moreover, there's a daily walk with two English Whippets through the leafy and pine-clad neighborhood, and always the tactile, sensory work each evening in my kitchen to create a fresh, organic, and nourishing meal for the nightly candlelit supper.

Despite it all, I'm feeling restless, blue, or burdened—sometimes all of them at once. Irrespective of my on-again, off-again yoga practice and the deep-tissue massage last week, I am slightly stooped and shoulders remain rounded inwards. Guarded. Contained. Rigid.

It's a strange paradox that delivering our soul work in life often requires us to be engaged with the so-called "real world" in challenging or merely tedious ways: hours at the computer, social media, networking and promotion, et al., which tend to feel decidedly soul-less. Like so much of life, the key seems to be in finding balance but, alas, I've dropped the thread again.

"I think you're part plant," a friend said to me a couple of months ago. "That's why you're so sensitive and why you prefer trees to people."

I could only chuckle in appreciation at her observation, knowing she meant it as a compliment. She's a wild soul herself, often more feral than fashionable.

Partially plant or not, I droop when too long planted in the domestic garden. I wonder, with merely tending the hearth and home, what sort of Green Man—that bearded, wild, Old World archetype of the Sacred Masculine—am I lately? When was the last time I disappeared amongst the pines, oaks or redwoods for an entire afternoon? Or followed a faint deer trail through a sunny meadow or the fragrant underbrush? Foraged and gathered a bushel of wild miner's lettuce for my dinner?

I need to set work and burdens aside and get out of town, wandering barefoot in an untamed locale for a while. Much as I enjoy ambling along the alluring shoreline, I usually don't wish to be at Point Lobos State Preserve, which is nearly always too crowded and "loved-to-death," as my park ranger friend puts it. And I remain caught in a conflicted relationship with majestic and wild Big Sur, as shared in the first post of last year's 3-part series, "Leaving My Shoes Along the Trail."

My solution is Garland Ranch Regional Park in Carmel Valley, a roughly 4500-acre preserve stretching from the willow-lined river along a cotton-sycamore floodplain, up into a wild expanse of hills covered in oak and chaparral (an alluring redwood canyon rewards those who go far enough). Though it's a favorite hiking spot among locals, I've kept mainly to the coast and not wandered there since late autumn.

The past two weeks have felt like spring, at last. Everywhere in town the trees explode into colorfully scented fireworks, and formerly bare branches now leaf out with tender green eruptions. As a gift of the abundant winter rain, a thick carpet of green grass and flowering weeds covers the land, and this stretch of the coastline is currently so lush and verdant it looks more like Ireland than typical parched, brown California.

At 61°F (16°C), the day feels warm enough that I decide to leave my light jacket in the car beside my boots. Unclad soles on damp, gravelly earth, I cross the unpaved, nearly empty car park and it occurs to me that the seasonal foot bridge might still be removed due to the winter/spring level of the river. Indeed it is, and the sign blocking the path says the occasional bridge won't be reinstated until April. So I walk several hundred yards west from where I've parked, down to the main crossing, listening to the gurgling voices of the rushing waters just a dozen feet away.

Two years ago, needing desperately to escape Honolulu and O'ahu, I rented my first little California *pied à terre* in Carmel Valley. Perched on a southerly hillside, the studio was little more than a converted garage with a small kitchen and bathroom, but it suited my needs and modest budget for a writer's retreat. Perched on a hillside, what it lacked in amenities and furnishings was compensated by a lovely view. Evenings found me bundled up on the deck with my rapidly-cooling supper, a glass of wine, and a flickering candle in a purple glass holder. As the noise of the valley road gradually diminished, I could hear the river singing from a quarter mile away, accompanied in late spring by frogs serenading at night.

Walking today beside the clear, cold waters, listening to the high notes and low notes as the river rushes and shimmers amid the mostly bare trees, a soft *pang* in my heart belies how much I have missed the gentle song of my sparkling, wild friend.

Winter feels like it is finally on the run, and the willows all along the muddy bank are liberally brushed with new green in an almost audible sparkle of life. Yet much as I love the waterway, I don't fancy the noise of the road, so once I have crossed over the bridge, rather than ramble the riverside trail, I head across the freshly sprouted floodplain to get away from the highway. Treading barefoot in the tender green grass, savoring how good it is to be out of town and wandering solo, a smile breaks across my face. Overdue, this gentle re-wilding of myself.

Ambling beneath a cerulean blue sky strewn generously with white puffy clouds, my shoulders rolling back and chest opens again. At midday, the deer are sheltered among the trees and I haven't seen them, but I have noticed and followed their cloven tracks in the soft earth. There isn't any miner's lettuce (Clayfonia perfoliata) here on the plain, the tender green, vitamin-rich plant prefers a shady hillside, but I've plucked a few weeds that called to me and nibbled their astringent bitterness like a wild, foraging creature. Early spring medicine.

Eat the wild. It transforms you.

I haven't been strolling even half an hour when I realize that my entire existence has shifted. Smiling, I feel happy, my body awake and energized. Certainly it helps that I'm away from power lines, cell phone towers, neighbors' WiFi, and the pervasive, invisible pollution that makes life challenging for one who struggles with electromagnetic hypersensitivity (EHS). Yet the shift I feel is also something more than exercise, good as that is: the power of being in wild nature is working its way through my soles into my very cells, breath and soul.

The playful, curious, childlike part of myself feels near to hand, the one who is utterly content to crouch down and consider the wonder of a miniature pink flower at my unclad feet, or wander over to a gnarled oak and lay hands upon its rough bark, gazing up at the great spread of moss-hung boughs and branches. (The archetypal energies of Child and Wild Soul are closely related, I think.)

Life grabs and clutches at us all, piling details and demands high on the plate. Apart from work, there is always something insisting to be done *now*, today. And how easy it is to set aside those seemingly less-important elements, rituals, and self-care that really nourish us. At what cost...?

Following a narrow deer track through wet grass, my feet muddy, I decide, *I need to do this much more often*. Make time for it. Weekly at the very least, as with my Friday morning ritual of shopping the farmer's market at the college in Monterey. There are semi-wild places like Garland Ranch within ten minutes of my doorstep, and while it requires driving to reach them (the factor that usually deters me), I owe it to myself to get out as part of my self-care.

Lulled into the techno-trance of modern life, how quickly and easily we forget what's real and who we really are. *Wildness and nature are not luxuries*; they are essential to my well-being, especially as a conscious soul.

It is only when I am open and expansive in body, mind, heart and soul —as I am here and now beside the river, viscerally connected to something much larger and wilder—that I embody my best self. That one who is able to love and receive love freely, fiercely, and with abandon. Unplugged and unbound is when I am most welcoming of mysterious grace; better able to follow the golden, glimmering thread that leads me onward in life, even through underground passages and darkly tangled woods of my own psyche.

How do we re-wild the heart and soul? For me, it is always in those places where a million, invisible fingers of Nature softly pry off my hardened armor and calcified shell, unlocking my *essence*. Barefoot on unpaved earth, beside a singing river or among the graceful trees, that is where and how I always come home to myself—the real and not-so-secret self.

Friend, step outdoors and play. Go further than your front garden, allotment, or neighborhood park. Take the damn car and get out of town to rewild yourself—even a little bit, for a couple of hours. Kick off your shoes. Cast your senses ajar. Unchain the wild soul. For amid a million distractions of the modern world, it is often only when fully immersed in the wordless, sensual, living realm that we remember our one, true imperative as beings of nature:

Grow.

❧ ❧ ❧

A Bowl of Peas

(June, 2014)

It was a meal of utmost simplicity. Purity, even.

My partner had just departed for Europe, going on a few days ahead of me, while I lingered a bit longer in rural Carmel Valley on the central California coast before joining up together in France. It was early afternoon on a warm, sunny day and, driving back to my rented writing retreat, I decided to pull over at a roadside organic farm stand, one that I had passed multiple times before. On each of my visits to the valley, I had considered stopping to poke around a bit and see what they had on offer. Today was finally the day.

In the dusty unpaved parking area, I parked the car near a chest-height, colorful commotion of sweet peas along the fenced garden plot—a rowdy extravaganza of fuchsia, light and dark pink, and cranberry-colored blossoms, their curly green tendrils interwoven through the fence. Gorgeous, I thought, I'll snap a picture. Stepping from the vehicle, still a dozen feet away from the blooms, I was immediately hit by their sweet, intoxicating fragrance.

Marveling that I could smell the flowers from such distance, I walked over to examine them closely and bury my nose in the exuberant riot of sweet pea sensuality. Heavenly.

Walking into the Earthbound Farms roadside shop—erected not far from the field where the two founders initially grew lettuces, from which they built an organic produce empire recently sold for $600 million—I browsed the selection of local produce available. Along with an array of gourmet food items—jams, honeys, chutneys, chocolates, pantry items—there was the expected offering of organic lettuces, rainbow chard, kale of different varieties, carrots, onions, celery, peppers, zucchini/*courgette,* etcetera, all of which looked tempting and appealingly fresh.

Browsing the refrigerated wall of produce, considering my options for supper later on, oddly what beckoned me was the farm basket of English peas. They were screamingly fresh—so vibrant that I swore they radiated a subtle, invisible glow, as if they had only just come from the field minutes before.

Mind you, peas are not something I would normally gravitate toward. As a vegetable, I've never adequately experienced their fresh goodness. This wasn't helped by my recent years living in England, where this vegetable is terribly popular (a matter of national pride, even), most often served as "mushy peas" (that's actually what they call them)—generally an unappealing, lurid green, overcooked mash, frequently served alongside fish and chips—and I still failed to see (or taste) their appeal.

Yet the freshness of these plump pods was undeniable. Having recently traveled from Hawaii, where the seasons are negligible (along with any change in fresh or semi-fresh produce), I was in the mood for some California spring cuisine: favas (broad beans), globe artichokes, strawberries... even peas. Unsure exactly what I would do with them but unable to resist their sparklingly crisp allure, I scooped up a couple of large handfuls and placed them into a paper bag.

A few hours later, having recently nibbled on some good olives and aged, raw Manchego with a glass of wine, I stood in the small kitchen of my rented hovel and contemplated supper options. Not feeling overly hungry due to the early evening snack, and having no one to cook for but myself, yet still desiring something fresh and full of spring goodness, I decided that I would prepare the peas. *À la carte.* Meals for myself are often quite simple and I adore bright clean flavors, so this would probably hit the mark nicely.

Soft music playing from my iPhone plugged into countertop speakers, a glass of Oregon Pinot Gris standing nearby, I emptied the bag of fresh pods onto the counter. All the vibrant jade crescents had a slight sheen, almost waxy though they were organic. Startlingly crisp. In a relaxed manner, I began shelling them into a white French bowl, feeling utterly content in the simple, somatic meditation of the moment: the quiet pop of pods opening beneath my fingers, the toothsome green crunch when I would bite into one and marvel at its sweetness. As I worked, the scent that rose to greet me was vegetal, fresh, almost herbaceous––the smell of fresh spring and new life.

Chefs, cookbook authors, and cooking writers—myself included somewhere in the bunch—prattle on about "fresh," but that word conveys different things to different people. Salad greens in a sealed bag or a plastic clamshell container at the grocery store constitutes *fresh* for most people; picked days or even a week (or more) ago, the majority of produce has already traveled uncountable miles. Despite that those leaves are still (hopefully) green, such food is nearly dead, for as I have written in a previous post:

> *"There's also that invisible but nevertheless real quality, the 'life force'—called by various names such as* prana, Qi, mana, shakti, chi, *etc.—that always seems to*

be minimal (or absent altogether) in commercially prepared or packaged food. When you are accustomed to eating very fresh foods that are close to the source and full of prana, you immediately notice the difference when it's not there."

Fast food chains promote "fresh" in their slogans and advertising, at which I can only roll my eyes. *Save me, please.*

Admittedly we eat very fresh at our house, as locally sourced as I can manage—not always easy nor is there much diversity in Hawaii—which is why I love being now on the West Coast of the States. Still, I marveled at these gloriously fresh peas. They might only be trumped if I stepped out into a garden (which, alas, I still don't have) and plucked them from their curling vines and then returned to the kitchen to cook them. (I will admit to unabashed envy of my friends with gardens or allotments who are able to do such a thing.)

Released by my thumb from their snug encasement—which looks curiously like an emerald butterfly when opened—the little malachite pearls tumbled softly into the bowl with a soft, staccato, random cadence. Vivid against the white porcelain, more than once I stopped my work simply to admire the visual appeal. It was an artist's moment, a culinary love affair. *Soul food.*

Shelling complete, still admiring the mound of gorgeous green peas in the white bowl, I debated briefly how to cook them in order to best showcase their impeccable freshness. I opted to heat them for the briefest minute in a bit of organic, unsalted butter, along with a pinch of fine *fleur de sel* and a little squeeze of lemon. Simple. Unfussy.

The iconic American food writer, M.F.K. Fisher, once wrote, "Every good cook, from Fanny Farmer to Escoffier, agrees on three things about these delicate messengers to our palates from the kind earth mother: they must be very green, they must be freshly gathered, and they must be shelled at the very last second of the very last minute."

Quite unwittingly, I had met all three criteria for success. Now, taste would tell.

Transferring the flash-cooked peas to a wide-rimmed soup bowl, I carried my utterly modest meal outdoors and sat at the small bistro table on the deck. The sky above the valley approached the golden hour, when fading light transforms the oak-studded hills into a vibrant scene that, if someone added some old stone buildings, could remind oddly of Tuscany. I never tire of sitting there. Whenever ensconced at my rented retreat, I contentedly spend peaceful hours on that deck simply watching the drifting clouds, lazily soaring hawks, the vividly zooming hummingbirds, while listening to the wind rustle in the trees with a gentle voice of the timeless.

A worn linen napkin in my lap, I took another sip of the nicely crafted wine and turned attention to my meal: *petits pois au beurre.* Honestly, even as a fairly accomplished Paris-trained cook, I was not in the least prepared for the surprise that awaited my taste buds. The peas were warm and just cooked through, tender but still toothy. They were sweet in an appealingly green way, with just the right hint of salt and acidity from the lemon, all lightly bathed in fragrant butter.

"Oh my god," I said aloud to no one but the little birds, gnarled oaks, and evening breeze that flirted with my unruly hair. (The same words would fly from my mouth a week later in Cannes, when I stepped onto the street with a crusty, artisan *levain* baguette and tasted the end of it, a very different sort of taste experience but also heavenly.)

How cliché to say that each bite of peas was a revelation but, truly, it was. Those spanking fresh little jewels were divinely, insanely good. I sat and ate them unhurriedly with a wide spoon, chewing slowly, marveling at the superb taste and feeling a soft opening of my belly in a somatic response akin to joy.

Peas are *fantastic.*

Lingering in my state of gustatory bliss, I wondered, what could possibly follow *that?* There was only one possible answer: organic strawberries purchased the day previous at the little farmer's market in Carmel-by-the-Sea.

For the record, I don't waste time or money on those industrial-sized, California jumbo berries, the ones grown simply for size versus taste, built to simply endure the rigors of travel. These at the market, however, were not those. Smaller, and possibly an heirloom variety. Hopefully worthwhile, they certainly smelled alluring and delicious.

Indeed, they were, and I'd eaten half the punnet upon arriving back at my writer's shack with them, but the remainder still waited in the fridge. I stood and cleared my empty bowl from the table, walked back indoors where I placed the chilled strawberries in a small decorative dish, and then returned to the deck. I'll let them warm a bit, I thought, but as I watched the slow arrival of a painted dusk, I couldn't resist. One by one, I ate the cool red berries, relishing the explosively ripe (if a bit too chilled) flavors of springtime in California.

It was the simplest of meals and yet beyond satisfying. It could only have been better if I'd had someone to share it with—though then we would probably have wanted something besides merely peas. Gazing out on the evening mood of the rural valley, noting that the recently green hills were rapidly fading to summer brown, I savored the feeling of total wellbeing in body and soul, all my senses fed and heart open wide.

Gentle reader, you know that I'm repeatedly asking, *what nourishes the soul?* Certainly good, fresh food constitutes a part of the multifaceted answer, and when we can eat in an environment that gently delights the senses, so much the better. Pleasure, beauty, awareness, goodness, and gratitude all feed our core essence of self. Immeasurably so.

Soul Artists appreciate food as something more than a reductionist equation of carbohydrates, protein, fat, calories, vitamins, minerals and phytonutrients. Appealing fare is a sensual affair that soothes the deep hunger of the soul for authenticity and connection—to place, to each other, to the seasons, to earth—as surely as it delights the taste buds. And when the meal is truly fresh and promotes health, we move closer to wellbeing on a deep, indescribable level.

As the Northern Hemisphere tilts fully into the axial phase of earthly abundance, here's hoping that you'll find something fresh and appealing—ideally also local and organic—and consider making yourself (loved ones, too) a simple meal of purity and goodness. See if you can locate something fresher than what's offered at the supermarket, perhaps from a farmer's market or farm stand. (If you are blessed enough to have a garden, I salute you... and I'm coming over for dinner.) Even if it is only a bowl of glistening ruby cherries, may that vitality stimulate dulled taste buds and fill your cells with a sense of life force––the source from which true health always arises.

Life is good, especially when it's *delicious.* Now imagine what it is like to thrive. Knowing that there is nothing better for body and soul that you could do, I wonder, to what fresh, simple meal will you treat yourself and the ones you love?

❧ ❧ ❧

Men and Beauty: Evolving the Masculine
(May, 2014)

"**Y**ou probably want this on a pretty plate..."

A faint note of sarcasm or weary condescension colored my friend's voice as she stood at the stove and peered into the steaming pot of homegrown beans she had just cooked.

"I know what you're going to say," she added, still in a patronizing tone, "you don't like the brown beans in a brown bowl."

Her husband was still away on his latest trip, and the two of us were in the kitchen preparing a simple supper.

"Absolutely correct," I smiled, giving a final stir to the sautéed greens under my command, freshly harvested from their garden. "Of course I want it on a beautiful plate."

Turning from the shelves where the everyday brown crockery was stacked, she opened the glass cupboard containing Tuscan-style ceramics, and set two wide-rimmed, yellow, hand-painted bowls on the kitchen counter. Into each attractive vessel I scooped some of the piping hot Anasazi beans and then piled the flash-cooked greens atop, their enticing aromas of garlic and lemon wafting up to seduce us.

Each with a glass of local Pinot Noir, we sat in the small, window-clad dining room to enjoy our simple rustic fare.

"You are one of the three most particular people that I know," my friend muttered as she lit two taper candles on the table, "just behind my sister. I'm not sure who the other one is, but you are certainly in the top three."

I smiled at the remark, ignoring the slight edge to its tone, and shrugged.

"Food should always look beautiful," I said, placing the cloth napkin in my lap and reaching for the garnet-hued wine to swirl it round in its glass.

"If you take the time to prepare a nice meal, even a simple one like this, it deserves a good plate. And yes, I am *very* particular. Details matter to me. A meal is a multisensory event, more than just *taste*, and I appreciate the nuances of all the elements involved—an attractive dish, a proper wine glass, a cloth napkin, some nice cutlery. Candles. A quiet space to enjoy it. Sitting down to eat at the table. It all adds to the experience."

She smiled at me with a tired look in her eye, as if she was just slightly amused at my apparent fussiness. I clasped her hand for a moment of silent thanks and we both dipped into the beautiful, broad bowls in front of us.

℘

In the time since that late summer dinner, my thoughts have often circled back to her comments about my desire for eating in beauty. Although some people might see it as fussy or precious, it's actually so much more than being *particular*.

I'm a man who appreciates beauty on many different levels. As a French-trained cook, preparing something to eat goes beyond simply getting food on a plate (although I will admit to moments of being ravenously hungry, or crashing blood sugar levels when appearances don't matter much). And daily I admire the ever stunning display of nature, often stopping to behold a colorful flower, the graceful shape of a tree, a small weed, wild bird, or whatever catches my eye. I cultivate beauty in my home environment, too, each thing carefully considered not only in its materials, look, craftsmanship and *feel*, but also its placement in the room or space.

On some level, I've always been this way, even as a child. Most young boys, playing in the dirt with their model fire trucks, want to grow up to be firemen; I liked arranging flowers and wanted to be a florist. A bit later, I wanted to be a musician and a writer, but I always liked making things pretty and nice.

Since my earliest days I've been attuned to the sensual texture of things: a moss green velvet shirt I wore until the elbows were threadbare and it was two sizes too small (when my mother finally confiscated it), a loathing of the fuzzy skins of peaches, a keen fondness for silk and fine linen, an appreciation for complementary colors, a preference for soft-soled moccasins or to be barefoot on the earth.

In the last couple of years, I've also begun paying attention to beauty in a more focused way—consciously celebrating it. Through the long process of writing a book that centers on *eros,* an evolved masculinity and the soul, I realized that beauty nourishes us on a very profound level. I'm referring here to elemental beauty, as in nature: the sort that might arise from an artist's craft but can never be fabricated or commercially produced. Authentic, natural beauty opens us through our senses—embodiment—which is one of the requisites for a conscious, evolving life.

❧

Western culture has widely confused superficial glamor with true beauty; the first merely fluffs the ego, while the latter evokes resonance in our soul. Real beauty isn't about "design" or style, it emerges from somewhere deep within.

To the ancient Greeks, Eros was the god of desire, the son of beautiful Aphrodite. As a handsome and alluring divinity, Eros embodied the masculine aspect of love, a powerful deity in his own right. Sometimes regarded as a male fertility icon, the god of desire personified the energies of lust and intercourse, as well as beauty and love. To the Greeks, appreciating beauty was inherently part of the masculine.

Yet somewhere along the way in the past couple of millennia, we seem to have largely lost that key element of Eros, ceding the male celebration of beauty to artists and gay men. At what cost, I wonder.

Beyond our physical gender, each of us embodies so-called masculine and feminine traits in varying degrees. Because our society has essentially relegated the appreciation of beauty to the role of the feminine, however, men are uncomfortable claiming and celebrating it. Apart from the natural exquisiteness of nature—say, a stunning coastline or painted sunset—most men act as if they cannot recognize prettiness other than in the form of an attractive woman, as if it lessens their very manhood to do so.

How limiting and stereotypical to say, "Well, he appreciates beauty because he's gay." Such a comment perpetuates the myth that straight men don't or can't appreciate beauty. It has nothing to do with our sexual preference, really. And if only women and gay men are the celebrants of fairness and grace, men will continue to be estranged from their wholeness and authenticity.

Appreciating natural, elemental beauty is one of the most important things we can do in this life. It's a soul practice, actually.

Yet amid the nearly constant technological distractions of the modern world, beauty has to be utterly astounding to grab our notice—to somehow cut through the television, radio, phone calls, barrage of text messages and emails, daily drama and endless mental chatter. Most of us are simply not paying attention.

Beauty is everywhere, from the untamed wilderness to the solitary blade of grass pushing up through broken concrete in an inner city neighborhood. We simply need to open our eyes and hearts. And with only a modest effort, we can create it ourselves in our environment and life. Even if it's only dinner. Or the manner in which we sit down to enjoy it, shared or solo—on a beautiful plate by candlelight.

I heartily salute the men—gay, straight, and those dancing somewhere in between convenient labels—who comfortably celebrate beauty where they encounter it. Or who take the time to create it in their personal surroundings and the world at large. It doesn't make us less of a man to appreciate beauty, rather it makes us an evolved, conscious one.

Brother, here's hoping that you find moments to pause and appreciate the beauty around you. Do it publicly. Openly.

I wonder, what was the most beautiful thing you witnessed today?

☙ ☙ ☙

*[This post was originally written for my once-and-former column on the Sacred Masculine for the **Good Men Project**.]*

After the Storm: The Gift of Losses
(July, 2012)

After twenty-four hours of hard rain, in the midst of a powerful and intriguing dream, the crash outside wakes me in the dark, predawn hours. It takes only a second for my sleepy brain to categorize the sound as a falling tree, though I am still disoriented enough that I cannot exactly place which side of the property on which it has plummeted. Not hearing any dreadful crunch of metal or shattered glass, nor any reverberating thud against the house structure, it seems that both car and cottage still remain intact, and I promptly roll over and drift back to sleep in hopes of recapturing my dream.

In the light of morning, stepping outside on the *lanai* to scope for the downed tree, I am greeted by a significant tangle of rearranged greenery and raw wood below the deck. A thirty-foot limb of one of the taller beings has fallen, taking out a number of smaller trees and their branches on its rapid descent to kiss the earth. No damage to house or property, however, for which I can only feel grateful. Just a good deal of fallen wood to cut up; a free delivery of new, uncured firewood.

Our little rented cottage high on the slopes of Maui's volcano, Haleakalā, is nestled in a delicately scented mixed wood of eucalyptus and pine (intermingled with spruce, cedar, and juniper), as well as other trees whose names I don't know. Given the strong winds that hurl across the upper mountain, meeting no other obstruction as they cross the open Pacific, we frequently lose trees up here—particularly the fragrant eucalyptus with their relatively shallow root system and weak trunks—sometimes blocking the road when they fall.

After morning tea and toasted slices of my homemade, hearth-baked bread, I venture outside to be embraced by the quiet, elemental energies of this refuge on the mountain; my morning ritual of standing barefoot on the earth and communing with the 'more-than-human' world. Casually, I wander down to inspect the fallen tree at the south-easterly edge of the wide patchwork of scruffy lawn.

Drawing close to the severed and broken limb, what strikes me immediately is the vivid, rust color of the heartwood, gradually becoming lighter and blonde as it reaches the periphery. I have the immediate image of bone marrow. The interior wood is pulpy, fibrous, and wet with moisture; any tree is essentially a wick for water, nutrients, and photons of light. The inner fibers are a far cry from the hardened, cured material that most of us are familiar with as *wood*.

Still caught in the imagery of bones and marrow, I muse how the inner texture is not dissimilar from the human body's bones, also perceived as hard and solid yet are actually somewhat spongy, permeated with liquid tissue, and composed of living cells. I bend down to smell the soft, wet wood up close, but there is very little scent—only something akin to wet cardboard. My hands on the roughly torn arm, I recall a solo hike years ago in the mountains of northern New Mexico after a violent windstorm, where the golden aspens everywhere had been snapped like toothpicks. It was there that I had first encountered the soft, fibrous innards of standing beings that are normally hidden from us.

I gaze up at the main tree's thickly corded ropes of rough bark, its great torso now shorn of a muscular appendage, reflecting upon how the loss has now changed the energetic *feel* of both the tree and this part of the property. Without the overhanging limb and the shade it offered, the space below now receives more light and feels decidedly more open, and two insights emerge from my observations.

I am reminded that what others perceive as our exterior—either visually, or simply through the persona that we project to the world—rarely reveals what is actually within. For better or worse, we are seldom what we seem.

The second thought is that there is always a gift in unexpected loss; sometimes we need to drop something old and weighty so that we can continue to grow upright.

Yes, sometimes storms carry an unlooked for gift in their intensity.

The evolutionary journey of an awakened individual is something more than just discovering a spiritual path or gaining higher consciousness; it is learning to authentically embody our soul, our unique creativity, and to offer that forth. The process of becoming ever more *authentic* is also a method and means of becoming more *transparent*: less layered over with protective patterns, ever more expansive, and more willing to be a vessel for the Deep Imagination that seeks to emerge *through* us. We all have weighty patterns and parts of ourselves ready to be released. Sometimes these elements may seem essential to who we are but, really, it's more likely that they are merely familiar rather than fundamental.

As we endeavor to awaken, transform, and grow as conscious individuals, we are repeatedly charged with the uncomfortable task of honest self-assessment: *How does this pattern serve me?* Does it support authentic growth, or does it help to avoid a more challenging and risky developmental task—such as being vulnerable, asking for what we really want, or learning to accept assistance?

Particularly as men, when we endeavor to move towards a more expansive and balanced embodiment of manhood, one that personifies the archetype of the Sacred Masculine—essentially a heart-centered and consciously interrelated manner of being—there is much of our protected, armored way of being that needs to drop away. Simultaneously, we must continue to draw up essential nourishment from our roots buried deeply in the earth and nature, deep creativity, the energetic potential of the body, and the mysterious summons of Eros.

Gentle reader, as your day and week unfolds, here's hoping you will recognize the storms and unexpected losses as cleverly disguised gifts and opportunities. May you be willing to sacrifice the parts of yourself—gnarly or beautiful—that hold you back or weigh you down. All while you continue to grow towards the light.

❧ ❧ ❧

Dancing the Soul: Sweat Your Prayers
(February, 2014)

The slight breeze is a heavenly gift upon my perspiring body. Having stepped outside into the open air to catch my breath and cool down, I gulp a few deep breaths, hands on my hips, heart thumping in my chest like a solid drum with rapid cadence.

For a few minutes I stand there, breathing deeply, and then step back through the door into the studio. Immediately, I am embraced by the compelling beat of evocative music, the humid warmth of bodies in motion, the slightly pungent smell of sweat, and a welcoming coolness of the wood floor under my bare feet. Reentering the large room of moving, dancing individuals, the thought or impression arises: this is a Temple of Souls.

It is Saturday morning and I'm at a movement studio in Santa Cruz, California, to join a free form, "ecstatic dance" event. It's the type thing I used to partake in regularly years ago when I lived in Portland, Oregon, when on weekends I would head downtown to the welcoming refuge of BodyMoves Studio. Sometimes my partner came along too. Together or solo, I would join the weekly communion of dancing, expressive, ecstatic souls in a 5 Rhythms class—a popular format developed by dancer and movement arts guru, Gabrielle Roth. I used to half-jokingly refer to my Sunday morning social dance as "going to church."

By the gods, I've been away too long.

It was years ago that I gave up yoga classes with their comparatively static sequences of *asanas* in favor of a movement arts practice—ever since meeting the alluring Roth in Denver and discovering her 5 Rhythms work. Through the past decade and a half, I have danced communally when lucky enough to find an open studio or gathering, ever relishing the shared energy, and I have danced on my own in the privacy of my house wherever we have roamed. When alone, sometimes dancing is simply a workout, while other times it is a moving meditation. Often it seamlessly fuses both. Regardless, it's always a portal to authenticity, and I've learned that nothing frees stuck energy like shaking it loose with movement.

The music quickly pulls me in again and my feet start moving, spine undulates, hips gyrate, my neck rolls loose and arms carve patterns in the thick air around me. Wearing some old hemp yoga pants cinched with a drawstring and t-shirt emblazoned with artistic waves and Hawaiian *honu* (green sea turtle), my body delights to be in motion; I am strong and powerful, if slightly rusty. I've been letting my hair grow out these days, looking slightly unruly, and the crazy curls of my salt and pepper mane are wet with sweat as I push them back from my face. With a slightly mischievous smile, I navigate the crowded space, circling and turning, occasionally catching someone's eye or exchanging a little grin, all of us disciples of the dance.

This is the realm of the wild demigod Pan, Eros, and Dionysus... not fair Apollo.

I drop deeper into the flow, letting my body explore new patterns. This sort of gathering isn't so much about *dancing* (e.g. steps, posturing and techniques) as it is simply a form of creative, somatic expression—allowing the music to seduce the *soulbody* and move in an authentic way. It is free, non-patterned and unformatted. Probably no one in the studio is a *real* or professional dancer; instead they are men and women of every size, body shape, character, constitution, temperament and sexual orientation—individuals who find themselves called to explore some aspect of themselves in collective dance. It might be for exercise but more likely they are here simply for the sheer enjoyment of group movement. Some are lithe, fit and graceful, others are not. No matter. Each one of us knows that little moves the soul like dancing.

At one point in the session, during a song that I don't particularly resonate with, I drift to a corner of the studio where I rest on the floor and stretch in a yoga-style pose to further open my chronically tight hips. As I gently move, roll, and stretch, a powerful sense of sadness washes over in a rugged, blue wave that drags me under. Curious, this, because I've been nearly giddy ever since I stepped through the front doors of the studio, bubbly with the excitement of coming home to myself.

I spend a few minutes simply *feeling* the emotion, allowing it to cascade and flow through me, observing where I feel it concentrated in my body—simply being with the very palpable sadness. From my hips and core, it rises and gathers in my throat; for a moment it feels like I could even cry, but then the sensation of sorrow behind my eyes abates and slips back down into my body, hiding again.

Tracking the affect, I realize that the core of sadness crystallizes around that I have let this very essential part of me—my luscious, ecstatic inner dancer who delights in sharing the communal ritual—be neglected for so very long.

How could I be gone from this for so many years, I wonder, but it is rhetorical. My absence has largely been circumstantial. With our move to Europe and tendency to settle in more rural areas, I've not resided in a place with an ecstatic dance gathering. (None that I could find, anyway, and I certainly did look.) This morning, once again in an open dance studio, I realize how profoundly my soul has missed the unspoken camaraderie and shared energy of dancing with others in this embodied fashion.

The past years as roaming gypsies in our painted wagon have yielded all sort of adventures and unexpected blessings; it has been a period of intense personal change and growth. But for the comfort of each other, our time living abroad— even our return to Hawaii—has mostly been a solitary passage, and as I have written elsewhere (and shared in a podcast or two) perhaps what we have missed most in the extended, nomadic wandering is *community.*

I've been musing (and writing) quite a bit in the past year on *passages,* how one's life is mainly a long series of them stitched together. Some passages feel easier or more joyous than others, and some prove distinctly challenging. Certainly, each offers inestimable gifts—*if* we are open to discovering and embracing them.

Mine is a hand-shaped life, one where I draw near to what beckons me and offer it the gift of my attention. As an artist (using that term broadly), my role is to notice with keen attention. Listen. Appreciate. Wonder. Expand. Create. Share.

And dance... preferably with others.

The Saturday morning gathering is a non-verbal zone, each week's dance centered upon a theme or dedication, and the intention offered for today is *Forgiveness.* As I deepen in "pigeon" pose and explore the velvet-soft contours of sadness, I choose to soften—into the stretch of my hip flexors, breath, my emotion, and also into self-forgiveness for the long absence from the Temple of Souls.

Soul is the most authentic, creative essence of an individual. Across cultures throughout time, the paths to discover, cultivate and celebrate that *élan vital* have included music, singing, chant, drumming, breath, storytelling, and dance.

Dancing frees, expresses, and nourishes the *soulbody*; it loosens our somatic armor and restrictive patterns. Indeed, as an archetype we would do well to court and cultivate the Inner Dancer, who may be the very best guide to the playful, powerful, sensual celebration of the lusciousness of life.

In our mostly soulless society, a modern day shaman might ask, *when did you stop dancing?* And can you lose your inhibitions enough to risk it again?

Gentle reader, here's hoping that you'll put on a bit of music and allow your body to move. It needn't be *dancing* and perhaps it's better if it is not. Simply allow yourself to explore movement with music, whether gently or wildly, to open and stretch and invite motion to sequence through your entire body. Try it just for five minutes and notice the difference in your bodymind—a sense of lightness and energy. Maybe you'll end up out of breath. No worries, that's just your body's invitation to do it more often. Perhaps you'll choose to dance with your beloved, your child, or the dog. Go for it.

If you're feeling very adventurous—and lucky enough to live where there's a communal dance studio—go move with others. Enter the Temple of Souls, surrender to the music, shed your inhibitions, and explore whatever seeks to emerge. Dance your edge(s), your familiar patterns of engagement or withdrawal, while celebrating and fully inhabiting the ecstatic resource we call *body*. Dance your anger. Inhabit your sadness through movement. Mobilize and express your joy. Reclaim and embody your Wild Soul.

Now that I've discovered my new "church" you'll find me regularly back here when in coastal California, dancing with a freshly found community of wild souls. Sweating. Celebrating. Barefoot on the studio floor, engaged with others and exploring the boundaries of contact—energetic or physical—dancing with authenticity, personal power and Eros. Shaking it all loose to the compelling summons of music.

Let your life be a wild love prayer to the Earth, the Sacred Other, and the Beloved. Dance your devotion, I say.

Or as Gabrielle Roth says, "Sweat your prayers." Amen, sister.

ॐ ॐ ॐ

Copper and Clay: Cooking for the Soul
(December, 2014)

It is a thing of almost unutterable beauty.

The elegantly curvaceous copper pot gleams in the light, looking decidedly Old World in both shape and craftsmanship. A gift from my beloved this Christmas, the hand-hammered *couscoussier* is one of those rare pieces that seamlessly melds form, function and beauty. I keep walking in to the kitchen simply to gaze at it sitting on the counter, admiring the way the burnished metal glimmers like firelight.

Technically, it's two pots in one: a rounded base pot for cooking broth, meat and vegetables, and an upper portion whose base is perforated for steaming couscous (or veggies). A *couscoussier* (pronounced "couscous-yay") is the time-honored way of making couscous, the essential Moroccan dish that many people think is a grain but is actually made from semolina, and thus more closely resembles miniature pasta. Couscous can also be made with barley, which was its traditional Berber origin before it was widely supplanted by wheat. Repeated steaming and breaking apart of the couscous (allowing it to cool and rolling it between your hands) is the secret that yields the fluffy, light texture you encounter in the dish at a good Moroccan restaurant (or anywhere in Morocco)—a characteristic quite difficult to duplicate at home when using substitute methods like simply hydrating the couscous with boiling salted water, or (blasphemy) zapping it in a microwave.

The couscoussier is the best sort of gift really. The elegant copper vessel is something that I have admired for years, but given its somewhat specialized use (to say nothing of the price tag) haven't splurged upon to buy for myself. That said, considering that Moroccan food makes a regular appearance at our dining table, the hammered pot will be in my kitchen for a long, long time, especially in light of its beauty and craftsmanship. Gorgeous and practical.

To my point, on Christmas Eve, having disembarked from a five-hour mainland flight to Hawaii earlier in the afternoon, we sat down to a homemade Moroccan *tagine* of free-range chicken, olives, and preserved lemon, with a saffron-infused rice pilaf served alongside. Decidedly non-traditional for a Christmas time supper, yes, but oh so delicious. It is the sort of fare that I generally like best: uncomplicated, comforting, and rich in flavor.

Taken a step further, when prepared with tools, pans and dishes that yield delight in their use, design and feel—like a copper couscoussier or a clay tagine—the work of such a meal becomes a delightfully tactile, soul-nourishing process from start to finish.

Nigel Slater, a popular food writer in the UK whose "cookery" books I enjoy, when discussing the tools and "kit" of what one needs (or doesn't) in a kitchen, states, "... I don't know anyone who has used their Moroccan tagine more than twice." It's rare that I'm at odds with Mr. Slater but I adore my clay conical pot, and employ it regularly. Further, I'll confess to owning two. Handmade and hand-painted, I truly appreciate their little differentiations and imperfections (rather like us humans, one could say).

There is something elemental about cooking in clay: earthy and timeless. Generous and old fashioned. It's the antithesis of everything slick, high speed, impersonal and mass-produced in our world. Yes, it requires a certain care and mindfulness, and an unhurried approach, but that's not a bad thing. Quite the opposite, I would argue. Even after its initial *curing* (soaking in water overnight, placing it in an unlit oven, and then slowly heating the pot for a couple of hours), clay vessels need to be warmed slowly so that they don't crack; clay doesn't like thermal extremes, and care must be taken not to set the hot pot on a cold counter (or any other similar kind of temperature shock). Yet there is a quality to food that has been slow-cooked in clay that I can only describe as nearly magical, or to utilize the *single most* overused adjective in food descriptions today—most of them very far off the mark—"authentic."

Cooking with clay moves us back towards the realm of soul. A few years ago, I owned a *cazuela* from Spain: a round, glazed casserole in which I cooked all manner of good things. Alas, it met a tragic and premature end, and I've not yet found a suitable replacement. I treasured its feel, earthy hue, and graceful shape. Like the tagine, whatever I cooked in it possessed a beguiling charm, depth of flavor, and visual appeal that other non-clay vessels fail to replicate.

"Have nothing in your house that you do not know to be useful, or believe to be beautiful," said William Morris, noted textile designer associated with the British Arts and Crafts Movement in the mid to late 1800's.

Placed side-by-side on the counter, or stovetop, my copper couscoussier and the clay tagine(s) are functional works of art. Each does an unparalleled job with what it was designed to do, while offering a tactile, sensory delight and beauty in the process. What more could one wish, really.

Those who read this journal on a regular basis know that I'm frequently prattling on about the simple pleasures of the day—particularly those in the kitchen, or gathering at table—and being fully ensconced in the sensuality of the moment. They are the simple celebrations of being human, I say.

Both in this column and *The Bones & Breath*, I've spent a good deal of words on the response in the heart—and body, generally—to what is presented to our senses. How does it *feel*? What happens in the bodysoul when we touch a thing, either physically or with another sense, or feel its touch upon us: an expansion and opening, or a tightening and restriction? How does a room, or our house *feel* to us? For that matter, how does your life *feel*?

I cannot say that a copper or clay pot actually warms my heart, not in the way that a living thing does like a small bird, a beautiful tree, or the familiar hand of my beloved, but there is a subtle, somatic sense of *goodness*—a softening in my belly, a relaxation of the eyes, a caress of jagged edges, a gentle ease—which is what this Soul Artist is usually seeking.

Soul Artists are keenly attuned to the feeling sense of life. Indeed, *feeling* is a primary navigational sense, and they value the intuitive guidance of the heart and kinesthetic knowing of touch as much as logical mentation (sometimes more so). We are highly attuned to environment and the details that compose it, from plants in the garden to furnishings in the home, to the very tools we use. Having the *right* paintbrush, pen, guitar, hand spade, knife or pan offers its own joy, each possessing some quality that is entirely subjective yet matters deeply.

Gentle reader, as I have queried before, *what is the art you make of your life?* My hope is that you possess a few special objects or tools that deliver a simple pleasure when using them—offering something more than mere functionality while inviting you to savor the moment, no matter how briefly. Whether it's a gorgeous design statement or a battered old thing, may the items you choose to make use of (perhaps wear) somehow stitch you a bit closer to the core sense of yourself, what you value and appreciate.

Moreover, in terms of deep nourishment for *bodysoul*, here's hoping that you have the opportunity to savor something cooked slowly in a clay pot, prepared by generous and kind hands.

❧ ❧ ❧

Polenta à la Marlena: Food for the Soul
(July, 2015)

"**S**tirring polenta counterclockwise is to flirt with calamity."

So warns author Marlena de Blasi, relaying old Umbrian kitchen superstition. For several years now, ever since reading *The Lady in the Palazzo*—the first book of hers I discovered, though it actually comes third in her series of memoirs—the words echo in my head each time I'm standing at the stove, stirring the pot. Clockwise.

It is a July evening and I have decided to make polenta for my supper. Most frequently made with coarsely ground cornmeal, the dish is a slow-cooked, thick and creamy pap that fills you up and feeds the soul with warming goodness. In some ways, it seems an odd choice for a summer meal, yet here at my little writer's cottage on the central California coast, as cool silver fog rolls in to shroud trees and houses, polenta sounds *just* right.

I recently enjoyed dinner at the house of some friends in nearby Carmel Valley where, seated out on the terrace, we savoured a fair evening as vividly coloured hummingbirds zoomed loudly about. As they often do, my hosts invited me to harvest some greens from their impressive organic garden that is currently bursting with all sorts of bounty. Netted to protect it from the marauding and ravenous wild turkeys, the chard and kale is a verdant riot of abundance. There is butternut squash coming in, with the promise of corn and tomatoes soon to arrive in copious amounts, as well.

Nothing, simply nothing, beats eating fresh from the garden or foraged wild. That indescribable but very real element—call it *Qi, prana, shakti, mana*, or simply "life force"—infuses the food and our body with vitality.

Polenta topped with sautéed, garlicky greens makes one of my favourite dishes; the sort of rustic humble fare that I prepare most nights and never tire of. Unfussy. Wholesome and delicious. With the gift of chard and kale direct from my friends' garden, life feels blessed with the best sort of abundance.

So it is that I find myself at the stove, cooking polenta in the Italian hammered-copper pan in which I normally make risotto—one of my kitchen rituals—stirring the stoneground organic maize only in a clockwise direction, and thinking of

Marlena de Blasi.

She's been on my mind lately, Marlena—or Chou, as she insists I call her. I'm reading her latest book, *The Umbrian Thursday Night Supper Club,* recently released in the UK and Europe, and scheduled to appear in America later this year.

The copy in my possession arrived earlier this week as a gift from Marlena, herself. We met unexpectedly in May—the crowning moment in a series of events so seemingly random yet woven together, our meeting could only be deemed as Fate, as recounted in an earlier SAJ post. [Read "A Paris Encounter: Meeting de Blasi"]

At the end of our chat that late afternoon at Les Deux Magots, the iconic Left Bank café, as the bells of St.-Germain-des-Prés tolled loudly, she promised to send me a copy of her newly minted book. Several weeks later, returning home to Umbria from her travels, she wrote a lovely email informing me that a *pachetto* was en route.

When the bright yellow DHL parcel arrived from Italy, I felt excited as a child on Christmas morning. Opening the box, I discovered that it contained not only the anticipated book (with a dear inscription to me), but also a rectangular, decorative tin—meant originally for Italian cookies or chocolate, perhaps. Prying off the lid, the scent of something buttery, sugary, and herbaceous goodness wafted up to entice me, even before I unwrapped the linen-clad, home-baked, broken up delight.

Crunchy with toothsome cornmeal, sweet with brown sugar, and beguiling with its combination of rosemary and anise seed, the creation is something between a crisp flatbread and a biscuit or cookie. It is neither *biscotti* nor a cake. Honestly, I'm unsure exactly what to call it—all I know is that the sweet, salty, buttery and herbaceous thing is utterly *delicious.*

Repeatedly I have gone into the kitchen and opened the tin, breaking off another piece of the addictive goodness inside. Greedily, I've gobbled up the sweet, crunchy crumbs, licking them from my fingertips, shaking my head and chuckling in disbelief. *Marlena de Blasi—Chou—made this for me.*

As confessed in that SAJ post in May, I've often imagined her—a chef, food writer, cookbook author, expatriate, fellow sensualist—as something of a kindred spirit. We adore a certain style of rustic food, and although she never uses the word *soul,* in her own way, often she is writing about that very human essence.

Mind you, I was making polenta long before I encountered Marlena's books, and given a background in Ayurvedic cooking and healing, am always stirring in one direction—it's an *energy* thing. Yet many times, as I've tended the creamy golden porridge at a low simmer—moving the wooden spoon only clockwise—I've imagined us cooking together. Or gathering up fine, fresh ingredients at market somewhere. Such an alluring fantasy.

I made polenta last week as well, when guests from Wales confessed that they didn't know what it was and had never eaten it. Oh dear, time for culinary education. I scraped the cooked cornmeal into a shallow baking dish, smoothed the top and allowed the porridge to set, then topped it with fresh buffalo mozzarella. After grilling in the oven just until the cheese was melted, I layered on slices of heirloom golden tomatoes and dressed them with a thick ribbon of Moroccan green *charmoula*—a lusty, unctuous sauce of fresh herbs, olive oil, garlic, toasted spices and a hint of anchovy, pounded together using a pestle and mortar.

Smiling, I watched our visitors devour every bite and nearly lick their plates clean.

Alone now for a few more nights before returning to Hawaii to join my beloved, I prepare the polenta in a traditional, soft-serve way, the manner I like best. The kitchen in this writer's cottage is modestly appointed, and as I ladle the thick yellow porridge into a cereal bowl, I lament once again that I don't have shallow, broad-rimmed vessels to hand—preferable for soups, risotto, polenta, pasta... anything and everything, really.

The dish is crowned with sautéed greens from my friends' garden, to which besides a generous amount of garlic I have added a squeeze of lemon, a few grindings of fresh black pepper, and a liberal pinch of chile flakes for heat and seductive intrigue. With a crackle and hiss, a sprinkling of warm, toasted pumpkin seeds garnish the affair, their earthy scent mingling enticingly with aromas of chiles and garlic. Nothing timid, here.

Lighting the solitary beeswax taper as I sit down at table, a glass of nicely crafted Oregon Pinot Gris to accompany, I silently give thanks for the meal—as well as the goodness of life, despite its challenges. For a moment, I gaze out the window at the misty evening, observing the fog trailing ghostlike amid the dark sentinels of trees in the neighbourhood.

Somewhere in the world it is summer, I muse wistfully.

Picking up the soupspoon, secure in knowing that I have stirred the polenta only in clockwise direction and thus hoping—trusting—that I may continue to avoid calamity, I dip into the warm deliciousness steaming before me.

It's a rustic supper very much worth savouring, the sort that nourishes the bodysoul. Moreover, in a rushed and hurried world, food that takes some time but not too much effort, asking only our attention with some gentle stirring, is surely part of the antidote. *Slow food,* indeed, and I am quite sure Marlena—Chou—would agree.

Buon appetito.

☙

Classic Polenta

Ingredients:

4 cups (1 litre) cold water
1 cup (165g) coarsely ground, organic cornmeal
¾ teaspoon sea salt
2 tablespoons (30g) butter
1 ½ oz (40g) genuine Parmigiano-Reggiano, grated, about ½ cup

Method:

Boil the water in a large saucepan. Add the salt and whisk in the cornmeal. Bring again to the boil, then lower the heat to lowest setting and simmer, stirring continuously with a wooden spoon for at least 20 minutes (arguably much longer, it will depend upon the grind of cornmeal you are using). Clockwise, of course. Cook the pap until the grains have opened up to a smooth texture, the porridge is thick and creamy, and pulls away from the sides of the pan.

Remove from heat and stir in the butter and cheese, along with a grinding of black pepper.

Serve immediately, drizzled with best quality olive oil and your choice of topping (see below). Alternatively, transfer to a buttered 9 x 13 (23 x 33cm) baking dish, allow to set, and then cut into triangles (convenient for grilling later, if you choose to).

❧

Sautéed Garlicky Chard

Ingredients:

one large bunch of fresh, organic chard
3 tablespoons extra virgin olive oil
2–4 cloves of garlic, chopped
Juice of half a lemon
sea salt and freshly ground pepper
generous pinch of chile flakes
Optional: organic pumpkin seeds, toasted, for accompaniment

Method:

If opting for the pumpkin seeds as garnish, place them in a small, heavy pan over medium heat, and toast until fragrant and browned, shaking the pan regularly to prevent their burning. They will likely begin to pop and expand. Remove promptly to a plate to cool.

With a knife, sever the chard leaves from their stalks and set them aside. Warm the olive oil in a broad pan on medium-high heat. Slice the stalks in ½-inch (1.25cm) pieces, chop the garlic, and add them both to the warmed oil. Add a pinch of sea salt and stir until all has softened a bit, a couple of minutes. Coarsely chop the chard leaves and then add them to the pan, along with the lemon juice, and stir until they have just wilted (though you can cook them longer, if desired). Add the chile flakes, a grinding of fresh black pepper, and adjust seasoning as needed.

Serve atop the polenta, garnished with the pumpkin seeds.

Cook's note: it is the garlic, lemon and chile that elevates the greens from being merely healthy and rather bleak to something utterly delicious.

❧ ❧ ❧

Finding Balance and Well-being:
Unplugging at Dusk
(September, 2015)

I don't generally buy magazines, yet every now and then something interesting catches my eye.

Standing in queue at Whole Foods Market, the latest *Paleo* magazine, a publication dedicated to the recently popular Paleo diet and lifestyle, drew my attention with the words on its cover: "10 Ways To Limit Your EMF Exposure."

How timely and curious. I've been struggling with my electromagnetic sensitivities lately—deciding to get rid of the WiFi in the house (we've purchased a long, shielded Ethernet cable instead), along with several other steps like shielding the so-called "smart meter" outside. Surprised to see such an article on the cover of what I thought was a diet & lifestyle magazine, I placed the periodical in my basket.

I'm familiar with the basic Paleo tenet: culture has completely transformed since our primitive beginnings, yet our basic human physiology has not. What we eat now is far from the diet on which we first evolved—most notably the addition of cultivated grains, legumes, and refined sugars. Much of what we currently consume makes for less than optimal digestion and nutrition (let's not even talk about the rising glut of highly processed foods). For optimal health, the idea is that we should return to what some anthropologists speculate we once ate, the so-called "Caveman Diet": meats, fruits, vegetables, nuts and seeds, eschewing grains and most carbohydrates/starches. That said, debate rages about what our prehistoric diet *actually* consisted of, and even within the Paleo community what foods should be allowed.

In an intuitive, non-dogmatic way, I've been following a vaguely Paleo approach since giving up wheat a couple of years ago. (No small step for one who trained in *patisserie* and artisan breads in France.) From my own experience, especially given some longstanding blood sugar issues, I've learned firsthand that I feel best when following a diet emphasizing vegetables and a bit of animal protein, rather than carbohydrates (which tend to break down quickly into sugar and make me wobbly). My weight stays in balance, too.

Despite a deeply held fondness for the comfort of risotto and polenta (evidenced in previous *SAJ* posts), my general way of eating embraces a low-glycemic, alkalizing approach—emphasizing quinoa, millet and buckwheat, which are alkalizing rather than acid-forming, and technically seeds not grains. I have browsed a couple of Paleo cookbooks while in bookshops, and more than once toyed with the idea of formally "going Paleo." Other than my semi-weekly dish of risotto, it wouldn't be much of a shift, really... or would it?

I've given up sugar and wheat. Not sure I can forsake risotto or polenta.

Seated at home later that evening, I found the article on limiting exposure to EMF's (electromagnetic fields) to be interesting and worthwhile; of the ten suggestions, I was already doing half of them. Flipping through the rest of the magazine, what struck me was the glowing health of everyone in the pictures (lean and fit bodies, bright eyes, clear skin). I learned that beyond the food and diet aspect, Paleo emphasizes natural exercise and movement (and play!), as well as *lifestyle*: the importance of good sleep for rest and regeneration, sunshine, de-stressing (yoga, meditation), and—the element I found most interesting—no illuminated screens after dusk.

A few weeks ago, I wrote a post on my struggle to find a balance with the hours I have to put into social media as I build my author's platform. I decided that I no longer wanted my online time to be the hours just before bed, having discovered that I slept better when I've not been at the computer before retiring for the night.

Quite unexpectedly, here was *Paleo* magazine supporting that very decision, and for the same reasons.

Multiple studies have shown that artificial light affects our pineal gland and levels of serotonin, which that structure in the brain converts to melatonin, a compound that encourages drowsiness and sleep. The levels of this hormone should naturally rise as the light dims, but in our ever-illuminated society, we're blocking this natural, sleep-inducing response, making sleep more difficult (to say nothing of our ever busy and distracted minds, which don't usually help the process). The increasing brightness of our screens (including television and electronic tablets) further disrupts the health-inducing feedback loops of the body, with the result that we are not only sleeping less, but less well.

Having sworn off social media at night during the previous month and appreciating the difference—sleeping more quickly, more deeply, and better dreams—reading the *Paleo* magazine has prompted me to go one step further: *no screens after dusk.*

If you read this post regularly, it's likely you know that I don't watch television. For years, the absence of TV has made for generally quiet, pleasant evenings in our household. Being off the computer, however, has significantly shifted the quality of those after-dinner hours for the better. Despite a large amount of work needing to be accomplished—juggling three weekly online columns, editing my newly written manuscript, and logging social media time to expand my "platform"— ending those tasks at dusk has given the past week a remarkably different feel. I've returned to reading books, working at my Navajo loom, sitting outdoors, or just listening to some music in the evenings. I've even done a bit of creative writing and editing work on printed pages while my partner types away at email.

Alas, with an absurdly overflowing work Inbox, my dear mate is still chained to the computer most evenings, sometimes until the very late hours, trying to catch up and clear out communications in order not to fall hopelessly behind. [Warning: do NOT become the Director of an international film festival, or you risk never seeing the bottom of your Inbox again.] For many people, email has become something of a curse, I think—or at the very least, a double-edged sword. Supposed to make our life easier, whether or not such is actually the case, it has effectively colonized vast chunks of our time. Moreover, there seems to be an increasing assumption (read, expectation) that we will reply to those messages as swiftly as possible, day or night, work hours be damned. For better or worse, my reach and following remains small, and so too my total amount of correspondence, thus I am can reasonably shut down the MacBook by suppertime. Whatever messages I've not yet responded to can simply wait until tomorrow (and social media can most definitely wait).

There is something gracefully old-fashioned in this "no screens after dusk" approach, and as a quiet, old-time soul, I appreciate it deeply. Reading books, writing, or weaving are all traditional pastimes that *nourish* me—not merely entertain or distract, like being online. And I'm rediscovering that not staring at a screen at night, over-stimulating my pineal gland and optic nerve, delivers tangible benefits.

As a Soul Artist, I'm always seeking to cultivate that which *nourishes*, as well as expands me through the senses in some way. In that earlier post on social media and finding balance, I wrote, "I launch my days in a very deliberate manner with a quiet morning routine—greeting the dawn barefoot, a cup of tea, a candle and resinous incense, several pages of longhand writing. Why on earth wouldn't I want an evening routine that feels equally nourishing?"

Challenging as it may seem, less time spent on electronic devices is *always* beneficial for body and soul. Unplugging at dusk feels innately right and good to me, a step closer to living with soulful poise, intent and wellbeing. *Living deliberately*, I like to say—like lighting a candle and stepping outside to listen to the wind as it dances and whispers amid the trees, feeling bare soles upon soft, yielding earth.

Life is a curious journey. I wouldn't have expected that picking up a magazine in queue at the grocery store would significantly change my life for the better, nor in such short order. Except for the social media bit, I thought my soul-centered life was fairly balanced and well-oriented already. Still, I appreciate slowing down further and finding another way to *unplug* when nearly everything in our culture encourages us to do the opposite: speed up, work harder, and stay virtually connected (to mostly irrelevant stuff).

I long ago embraced my inner hermit. Perhaps it's time for me to welcome my inner caveman, as well.

The Paleo tribe advocates that well-being is a composite of diet, exercise, and lifestyle. I definitely agree, but feel compelled to add that missing from that equation is *soul*—the innate, ineffable part of being human that gives deeper meaning to life. Finding ways to nourish the soul is *essential* for a true sense of wholeness, balance and well-being.

Unplugging from automation and technology, even briefly, day or night, is a good first step. (It's actually one of the seven Soul Skills in my book, *The Bones & Breath*; specifically, Soul Skill #7, "Disconnect to Reconnect".)

Friend, here's hoping that even if you don't swear off illuminated screens after dusk, you'll find other ways to unplug from the technological stream of life, ceaseless information, and distraction. Choose something instead that deeply nourishes you. Go ahead; be old fashioned. Rather than high speed, live at *soul speed*. Your life will feel immediately richer for it, and one step closer to balance.

❧ ❧ ❧

Aromatherapy and Ritual: Bliss for the Creative Spirit

(August, 2015)

I wake to soft morning light, a pale glow on worn linen curtains in the bedroom, the welcome of a summer dawn.

Pushing back the fluffy duvet and emerging from a warm cocoon of bed, the rest of the household still sleeps. Even the Sussex Duo, our two English Whippets. I make my way to the bathroom and from there to the kitchen where I add water to the blue enameled tea kettle and set it atop a hissing flame. Then I open the front door and step outside the greet the day, a jar of golden grains in hand.

Clad loosely in hemp yoga pants and a green flannel shirt, crossing the unswept deck, I feel the smooth coolness of wooden boards and dried, cylindrical cypress leaves beneath my bare soles. In a heartbeat, the coastal air wraps around me with an alluring perfume of woodsmoke—someone in the neighborhood must be burning an early morning fire. The scent drifts and intermingles with the resinous fragrance of Monterey cypress and a faint, salty tang of the sea.

Though it is only early August, for a brief moment, the cool temperature of the morning air and aroma of woodsmoke catapult me forward to autumn—though that scent might just as easily transport me to camping somewhere wild and sitting near the flames of a fire pit.

Our olfactory sense is *astounding*. Wired directly to the limbic brain, which is largely responsible for our emotions, smell bypasses the higher processing centers and affects us in an immediate, primal way. Situated at the top of the nasal cavity, the roots of the olfactory bulb—the nerves most directly exposed to our exterior environment—detect molecules of scent in the air we breathe.

Years ago, when I was actively practicing as an aromatherapist, I taught a 50-hour course at a local massage therapy college. Alongside the properties and benefits of essential oils, I shared with students the beneficial ways we can use scent to induce the "relaxation response" (either with clients or in our own lives): triggering the parasympathetic nervous system to become dominant, and releasing a flood of positive, health-inducing benefits. When we create a positive association with a scent (such as in bodywork and massage, an aromatic bath, sweet incense in a temple, the smell of onions cooking, etc.), the beneficial physiological responses can be prompted simply by encountering that particular aroma again.

Woodsmoke. Lemony-green scents of Monterey cypress. Marine-infused air. Each of these stirs something in my bodysoul as I stand quietly, welcoming the morning. In the hush of this early hour, I can hear the sea a half-mile distant, a welcome voice that fades in the noise of the day.

Barefoot on the earth, in my usual manner, I cast my senses wide and greet the holy—*everywhere,* in each thing I see. Setting down the jar, laying hands upon the grey, rough bark of the grandmother tree that watches over and graces each day with timeless, windswept beauty, I offer brief prayers. Opening the jar's lid, I scatter golden grains of organic millet along the deck railing and faded red bricks, food for the little winged ones who will soon arrive to feed, knowing I have brought their daily breakfast.

Turning back to the humble, rented cottage, I reenter the house just as the kettle reaches a boil and then set about making my requisite pot of cheer: a robust, loose leaf, black tea blend that my dearest friend in England regularly sends to me from The Tea Palace in Covent Garden, London.

Outside the windows, the sky brightens with a summer song, graced with whispers of pink and soft blue. If the gods are kind, perhaps the foggy "marine layer" will stay away (or at least very far offshore) for a change. I place the cast iron teapot atop a cast-iron warmer that holds a small candle, where it will rest through the remainder of my early morning ritual: lighting a beeswax taper and a stick of incense, penning the first creative sentence of the day on a clean sheet of paper (then folding it up and setting it aside as an offering), followed by some pages of longhand writing in a notebook as the day arrives more vividly.

Wooden match sparks to life with a sulphuric hiss, igniting a stick of piñon pine incense. I place the thin, glowing baton in a holder on the fireplace mantel (*chinmeypiece* my UK friends call it) and return to the table by the window, preparing to settle in and write. In mere moments, the first aromatic molecules fly across the room to reach my nose and the invisible smoke unlocks an immediate response in my bodysoul: a deep breath, a sense of opening and expansion, a peacefulness. Bliss, even.

For twenty years I have burned piñon incense, ever since falling in love with the pine's smoke when I first dwelt in Taos, New Mexico. During cold months (sometimes even on a summer evening), a fragrant spirit rose up from the piñon logs burning in kiva fireplaces in adobe houses, perfumed the sky and filled me with delight. It is a smell that triggers in me a profound sense of well-being—of being *home* in a place that deeply nourishes, rooted to earth and soul. The fragrant smoke instills a sense of *sanctuary*, reweaves my connection to spirit, and somehow invokes the most creative, authentic part of myself to come forward.

Ever since dear Taos, along with a candle and fountain pen, piñon incense has been part of my writing ritual. Occasionally, I run out of these precious resin sticks (mostly when I lived abroad and had to order them), and when I don't have their comforting scent in the house, I long for it—a sensual element lacking my life.

What an exquisite gift of nature, these scented resins that give a fragrant smoke. Similarly the scent-ual extractions from flowers, roots, stems, leaves and wood that we popularly call "essential oils"—a term that I think is curiously perfect, conveying both the essence of the plant along with its value in our life. At the risk of sounding overly dramatic, I sometimes think that I couldn't live without these healing gifts of nature. (Of course I could, but what a drab existence it would be, like living in a derelict, industrial section of urban warehouses without any sense of semi-wild nature but for straggly weeds.)

In a real sense, *everything* that sustains humans is a gift from the plants (mycelium and microbes, too), including the very oxygen we breathe. Yet ignorantly or selfishly we take it all for granted.

For a sensualist soul, being enfolded by natural "aromatherapy" is part of the deliciousness of life. Nothing synthetic, thank you, like all those horrid air "fresheners" (*deadeners,* more accurately) and cloyingly scented candles. Or commercial perfume. Increasingly, everything from dish soap to deodorant is scented in the most obnoxious, chemically fake way that dulls our senses rather than heightens them.

Perched by the front window I sit, fountain pen in hand and poised to write, inhaling the moment. It is fleeting, this wisp of smoke that triggers my sense of bliss. Soon the scent will mostly fade into the background as I habituate once again to its presence, the woodsy, balsamic notes diminishing until lost amid the other inputs of the morning and clatter of my thoughts. The Sussex Duo will rise to greet me with wagging tails and brightly dark eyes. Whether slowly or rapidly, the day will shift, pulling me into a different mode of work, duties, and social interactions.

Gentle reader, you know how these simple moments seduce and compel me to write about them. Everyday, life is well-stitched with little, ordinary minutes that, if we are paying attention, are really sensual celebrations of life—the fragrance of fresh rosemary crushed and chopped in the kitchen, the feel of a fine tool in the hand, the warm touch of our lover's fingertips, the sweet juiciness of a sun-warmed peach, a mosaic of dappled shade beneath a noble tree. Yes, I write recurrently about such things.

Across the room, a thin stream of smoke rises from the stick's glowing tip, a ghostly blue serpent spiraling up and outwards, finally disappearing as a fragrant prayer to mostly forgotten gods.

A new day beckons softly with unspoken promise. Too soon, the usual distractions and demands will carry me downstream from this quiet place but, until then, I am simply breathing in, breathing out. I'm savoring the sweet, smoky scent of a smoldering stick rolled in resin, the expansiveness in my chest and belly that it invites, along with a sense of the goodness of life—while realizing once again that nature's gifts are uncountable.

It may be vanishing and ethereal as piñon smoke, but I will offer something of value to the 'more-than-human' world today. Tomorrow, too. And every day henceforward.

Just as nature does, may we all give ourselves away in beauty.

Blessed be.

ða ða ða

L'Olivier: The Olive Tree

(May, 2015)

I wish this were made of olive wood.

Such was the thought that lingered in my mind as I stood at the sink, washing the stainless steel ladle I had used for scooping the evening's homemade soup (organic broccoli and potato, in case you were curious). Despite my aptitude as a cook, the kitchen at my little writer's shack in California is quite modestly appointed—it's a writing retreat, after all. Most of what I own, the tools and *batterie de cuisine* deliberately chosen over the years for both function and aesthetic appeal, are at home, not here. (Admittedly, a half-dozen key favorites actually travel back and forth with me, stashed in my suitcase.)

A couple of months ago, I realized that I needed a ladle so I purchased a simple, inexpensive, stainless steel one at the local Sur la Table kitchen store in Carmel-by-the-Sea. It lacks on charm but adequately does the job it was intended for. Since its purchase, however, I have added two very nice cooking vessels to my little *pied à terre* —a copper risotto pan, and an enameled Le Creuset pot. So as to not scratch the respective tin or enameled lining, both of these pans require something other than a metal implement. I employ a couple of bamboo and olive wood spoons and spatulas as my preferred stirrers, but this metal ladle requires a bit of attention and care in its use. The time has come to find something better.

A deep fondness for olive wood developed several years ago in the south of Spain, where we resided in a whitewashed stone farmhouse amid the olive groves of Andalucía. Arid, rugged, and drenched in light, it was a landscape deeply alluring to my soul, stirring something ancient in my bones like a gypsy's guttural song. Gazing towards the blue wedge of the Mediterranean in the distance, I felt expansive, open, and rooted to earth in a way that I never did beneath the clouded skies of England. Whether sitting on the wide, brick terrace sheltered by the grape arbor, or gazing out the kitchen window while I prepared our meals—looking out *any* portal of the house, for that matter—the eye encountered silvery green olive trees stitched across the land like a quilt.

> *"Any direction one turns, the olives and accompanying almond trees flash and dance in the warm breeze, capturing the eye with graceful movement, and reminding me to stop and breathe as they silently generate tons of oxygen, their breath becoming mine,"* I wrote in my journal.

As a welcome to the farmhouse, our landlords (the husband is English, the wife is German) gifted us a large jug of unctuous, golden oil, pressed from the olives of the property and surrounding hills. I nearly clapped with delight at this humble, earthy and fabulous present. Not only was it inherently useful and utterly delicious, it established an intimate bond with the land we resided upon—to say nothing of the trees themselves, gathered all around the house. Like eating fresh vegetables harvested from one's own garden, every time I used some of that precious oil, I felt a powerful, visceral sense of connection to earth and place. Repeatedly, I found myself looking out through the kitchen window and quietly—sometimes audibly—blessing those countless *olivos*.

On my long rambles through the mountainous *campo* (countryside), passing amid the groves along a dusty track, I watched the ongoing harvest—an orchestration of workers, errant dogs, ladders, rakes, and nets stretched on the ground below the boughs. Just a few months later, the first new leaves and tiny, pinhead-sized, creamy buds of flowers appeared in mass profusion, signaling another cycle of life. At night in a cold house, the bones of old, cut trees fueled the wood stove and gave us heat, and I further appreciated yet one more of the olives' many gifts to mankind.

More than once in this column, I have confessed my ongoing love affair with trees, and I suspect that if I could peer inside my heart, I would find a tree growing there. It is either an English oak, a windswept Monterey cypress, or an olive tree. Walking among them every day, I swiftly came to feel a deep affinity for those gnarled, generous beings. As I wrote in the closing narrative for the book manuscript I completed in Spain:

"In an ancient land where countless others have dwelt before me, numberless and unrecorded journeys have transpired with the cyclical seasons of this place. Those of us in the New World seldom have the appreciation that ages have passed of ancestors working the earth, gathering harvests, tending the cooking fires, making love, burying their dead, and watching the stars. The whitewashed pueblo (village) in the valley below this house has been a settlement since Roman times, and there are even more ancient Phoenician tombs in the hills nearby.

Not far from here, just above the Rio de la Cueva, is a stand of olive trees with massive trunks thicker around than five or six men, twisted into spirals like the corkscrews of titans. Even in a land of old, gnarled olives, these venerable trees are remarkable for their age. I call them the Grove of Ancients, a wise and wordless council of beings so aged that I am humbled by their very existence. People have piled stones, seashells, and small objects at their base, as if making offerings. Since discovering them, when I pass that way, I stop and scramble up the rocky slope to lay hands upon their roughly furrowed bark, immersed in their powerful energetic field, and imagine their silent stories that span the centuries."

The remnant of olive oil in clay containers has been carbon-dated at eight thousand years. The oldest living olive trees in Lebanon, Israel, and Crete are dated variously between four and seven thousand years old; along with the bristlecone pine in the American Southwest, this makes them among the oldest organisms on earth. That is an astoundingly long relationship between tree and humans, one that I find humbling to consider, and it always shifts my own little life back into proper perspective.

Last year in Provence, while accompanying my partner to the Cannes Film Festival, my main splurge was in a charming little shop of local food stuffs—*épiceries Provençal.* There I purchased some *herbes de Provence* (a staple in my kitchen that never lasts long), a hinged-jar of *fleur de sel* (a gourmet French salt) infused with black truffle, a woven market basket with leather handles (to replace the one purchased in Paris fifteen years previous), and a beautiful mortar and pestle carved from local olive wood. The trip to Cannes was my first return to Provence in many years, and I went with the quiet hope of finding a traditional, ceramic, Provençal mortar and pestle (a unique style and shape). Yet I was so taken with the beauty of the *bois d'olivier* (olive wood), along with the shopkeeper's insistence that for daily, regular use I want a wood mortar, not the less durable ceramic which can chip, that I happily discarded my original intent.

I recently brought that olive wood mortar and pestle to my rented writer's abode where it sits on the grey laminate kitchen counter like the practical work of art that it is—one that gets used weekly (my heavier ceramic and marble ones remain in Hawaii). I never fail to be captivated by the beautiful, swirling grained wood, the elegant shape of the bowl, and the pleasing way it feels in the hands when I work with it. (Add to this that it is unsurpassed for making *aïoli.*) For me, it is also a connection to the Provençal landscape—a place on earth that I adore—and a lasting gift of the remarkable olive tree, which has sustained humans around the Mediterranean for millennia.

Like the copper *couscoussier* and the clay *tagine* that I wrote about in a previous

SAJ post ["Copper and Clay"], I have a deep appreciation for functional works of art—things that do an unparalleled job with what they were designed to do, while offering a tactile, sensory delight and beauty in the process.

Which brings me back to the stainless steel ladle and how it falls short.

If you read this journal even somewhat regularly, you know that I'm easily captivated by the small pleasures in the day. Those little human moments, ones where I'm suddenly deeply engrossed in the sensuality of the moment and how it *feels*—including what is in my hands—are simple celebrations of life. The items that I use, and those with which I've surrounded myself, are well made, solid and durable; their visual and kinesthetic aspect, their heft and texture in the hand, brings pleasure. I will make an occasional bow to practical—the ladle at my Carmel Valley shack, for instance—but the aesthete in me ultimately wins over and wants something more appealing.

Previously, I've quoted William Morris, the influential textile designer in the British Arts and Crafts Movement of the late 1800's, who said, "Have nothing in your house that you do not know to be useful, or believe to be beautiful." A motto to live by, I think.

In a week, I will be arriving on the Côte d'Azur, returning with my partner to the yearly film market and festival in Cannes. Though I don't recall seeing such a thing last year as I wandered through the various shops around town, this trip I will be scouting for a ladle carved from local *bois d'olivier*. It would be the perfect sort of memento, offering practical delight and beauty for years and years to come.

Soul Artists know that little rituals of the day nourish the soul, moreover that they are important—imperative, even—for doing so. Those ordinary moments when we are fully present in what we are doing—chopping an onion, sweeping the porch, reading a book, walking the dog, making a proper cup of tea—and appreciating whatever is in our hand. A wine glass. Handmade cup. A fine pen. Garden spade or paintbrush. A ladle.

As I have wished before, gentle reader, here's hoping that you possess a few special objects or tools that deliver a simple pleasure when using them—offering something more than mere functionality, while inviting you to mindfully appreciate the moment, however briefly. Part of the beauty of natural, handmade objects is that often they can stitch us to something larger, whether that is the artisan's life and energy, a certain place, or the elemental material itself from whence the thing came—like the munificent olive tree.

To root down in seemingly harsh environs, to find the nourishment and water one needs, to be integral to a landscape and the web of interconnected relationship, to quietly shimmer with knotted and unique beauty, to generate fruit to give away year after year—may we humans learn a thing or two from *l'olivier*.

Le Pain Quotidien

(May, 2014)

Funny how a comment made in passing can remain unexpectedly with you for years.

"You have to break the end off your baguette and eat it on the way home."

Such was Roberta's instruction to me as we exited Maison Kayser, an artisanal boulangerie a few streets away from her Left Bank apartment, shortly after I first arrived in Paris for my school year at Le Cordon Bleu. My hostess, landlady, and *tutrice* of all things *français,* Madame Rivin's voice still rings in my ears whenever I'm in France (occasionally at other moments, too).

Today, heeding her words, as I step from a boulangerie onto a sunny street in Cannes, putting my sunglasses back, I tear the crusty tip from the small, golden *flûte* (a short baguette, but not to be confused with a *ficelle,* a skinny one) and pop it into my mouth. The crisp exterior shatters into a slightly sour and yeasty interior, revealing a satiny crumb and open structure. The taste is so good, my gait falters.

"Oh my god..." I whisper, as a flood of tasteful Parisian memories come rushing back to my mind and palette. It's heavenly.

As someone who has extensively studied bread baking, both in France and the States, I know a thing or two about artisan bread (and pastry). How sadly ironic that I seldom eat wheat in America these days. Our modern grain has become so intensely hybridized to promote higher, industrial yield—even organically-grown wheat—that it's no longer easily digestible. The grain we currently consume is entirely different from twenty years ago, and it's a world away from what our grandparents ate. I feel poorly when I consume it. (For an eye opening and potentially transformative book, read the bestselling book, *Wheat Belly: Lose the Wheat, Lose the Weight, and Find Your Path Back to Health,* by William Davis, MD.)

After a couple decades of lackluster, commercial bread, France is undergoing its own bread renaissance, and when I encounter an artisanal boulangerie on my travels, well, I can't really resist. Paleo diet be damned. And oddly enough, thus far I don't feel poorly or have digestive woes with European wheat. *Quel mystère.*

Crusty loaf extending from a long, narrow paper sack in my hand, I resume my steps along the bustling thoroughfare, turning right on busy Rue d'Antibes, still chewing the oh-so-flavorful, slightly tangy, tip of bread. At risk of being overly dramatic, it's *so* delicious and well made, I could almost weep for joy.

The past days of roaming, window shopping, and sitting at crowded sidewalk cafes, observing the international crowd here for the film festival, have left me feeling a bit restless. Ungrounded. I realize that my soul is hungry. Not simply for food (the gods know I've had plenty of it here) but for simple, rustic nourishment, the kind that sustains me at home. The daily bread of my existence, *le pain quotidien*, is a quiet connection with earth and nature, writing, little rituals, and a home cooked meal with fresh ingredients––food that is prepared with love and gratitude, and then shared ideally with my beloved or friends.

My former work as a chef aside, there is no denying that I'm a cook at heart. More than a week away from a kitchen and lacking the creative, sensory, soulful nourishment of cooking *le bon repas*, I start to feel disconnected from something essential. A bit flat or wilted, like a tender plant in a drought.

So today I'm headed to the main open market, the Marché Forville, "the belly of Cannes" in the heart of town. Truthfully, I made a bee line for it on my second day here, eager to be once again in a fabulous French street market; the only reason that I didn't go the very first day was that on Mondays it is a *brocante* market selling all sorts of bric-a-brac, which doesn't really interest me. I'm here for the food, thank you. One of the most renowned markets on the French Riviera, the Marché Forville sits at the base of Le Suquet hill in the old part of the city—*le quartier le plus ancien de Cannes*. It occupies a covered but open air building that was built in 1880 (replacing a cluster of old market shops), altered in 1934, and restored in 1993. The market sits in a *zone piéton* (pedestrian only), surrounded by cafés, boulangeries, and various shops.

The spring day is gorgeous and warm, and I'm dressed in a rumpled shirt of tan linen, green trousers, and a favorite pair of loafers, feeling at ease and, dare I say it, happy. Blissed out with my baguette. For despite my earthiness as a barefoot soul, this environment too is very much who I am. Stepping through the large arched entrance of the pink building, a bustling hive of activity greets me: long rows of merchants selling colorful displays of vegetables and fruits, fresh flowers, herbs and spices, olives, meat, cheese, fish, and more, with a crowd milling about.

I am thrilled to be here, drinking in the multisensory experience. Few things bring me as much joy as a fabulous market, whether a farmer's gathering in a car park or a vendors' venue such as this one (apart from a few purveyors and beekeepers, the sellers haven't grown or made their products, they have purchased them wholesale).

It's a noisy and neighborly affair. Some tourists roam about but mostly the patrons are locals, doing their daily or semi-weekly shopping. The sight and sound of slightly argumentative voices of the French housewives haggling on price, while others exchange recipes or gossip with the vendors whom they know well, it brings a smile to my face. Along with a basket of memories of living in Paris and my twice weekly shopping at the open-air *marché* at Place Maubert, just a stone's throw from Roberta's flat. In some ways, the Marché Forville reminds me of the bustling Atarazanas market in Málaga that I frequented when we lived in Spain, though the building in Cannes is significantly smaller and far less crowded (read another way, far more manageable). Sometimes I think I could chronicle my travels and adventures by the markets I have visited.

An English leather "man bag" slung over my shoulder (with notebook, fountain pen, and iPad Mini stashed inside) and still carrying the partially eaten baguette in hand, I slowly peruse the aisles, absorbing the spectacle of colors, scents, and commotion with wonder and delight. The smells of fish, fruit, and cheese all mingle in an olfactory riot that is not unappealing. In my typical style, I must wander through and look at everything before making a single purchase. I like to see what's on offer, noting the various prices for items I might be interested in (they vary a surprising amount), comparing freshness (quality varies as much as the pricing), and even considering the vendors themselves—whether or not they seem friendly, I like their look, etcetera.

What a wealth of riches, this pavilion. And how deeply I miss living on the Mediterranean... a wistful pang suddenly in my heart.

I'm tempted by the little cardboard cartons of glossy, ruby red cherries and plump little berries—*myrtilles, fraises, framboises*. The various vegetable vendors all carry the staples available year round (even if grown in a far away locale)—onions, garlic, peppers, carrots, celery, aubergines, courgettes, tomatoes, leeks, cabbages, potatoes—but I am drawn to the heralds of spring: small purple artichokes, favas in their long pods, fresh peas, and asparagus. The French go mad for white asparagus and piles of the ghostly things are everywhere in the market; the thick pale shafts with bulbous tips look decidedly phallic, all the more so because of their length, size, and because they are not green. I linger over open bins of delicate loose-leaf lettuces that I adore, heaping mounds of *mesclun, mâche* (lambs lettuce), and *roquette* (baby, Italian-style arugula). Too, I pause briefly at table of earthy *champignons,* at least a dozen different varieties of mushrooms, half of them are ones I've not seen since living in Paris, including "La Trompette de Mort," the black trumpet mushroom, most of them with price tags that are rather dear.

Some of this bounty is local but much isn't. Just as California and South America supply the States with produce that is otherwise out of season, Europe's year-round fruit and vegetables come either from southern Spain—where it is grown in giant, long poly-tunnel greenhouses called *invernaderos* that have covered the landscape of coastal Andalucía—or from north Africa. I'm only interested in what is local, snappingly fresh, and preferably organic, though there seems to be nothing in the market that meets that latter criteria.

In the refrigerated glass cases with meat and poultry, the skinned rabbits have their heads on, as mandated by French law—an edict from the war years when food was scarce, proving that the long lean body isn't a cat, to which it looks similar. I'm tempted by the plump, free-range chickens—*poulet fermier de Landes*—yellow skinned *(jaune)* or purple *(noir)*, noting that some are bio (short for *biologique,* the French term for organic). The fishmongers have their own section of the market with large, tiled, rimmed tables where the daily catch is piled on ice, nearly everything sold whole rather than filets: *dorade,* snapper, eels, squid, *rascasse* (scorpion fish), turbot, monkfish, mullet, mackerel, tuna (essentially the only one sold in smaller portions), and more. The glistening skin and clear eyes of the fish reveal their freshness, and nearly beg to find their way into a tasty *bouillabaisse,* the classic Provençal fish stew.

Oh, for a kitchen! Of all the things that I adore and miss about France, the glorious open markets are top of my list. Alas, after a shuffle of apartments within my partner's work team, giving them the larger flat, we have landed in a small studio *sans cuisine.* So despite this fabulous abundance of gorgeous things to eat, I have no means to cook, and we are reduced to dining out for nearly all our meals. For me, it's definitely part of the Cosmic joke—which, dear reader, is almost always on us. *C'est la vie.*

After a good while of simply browsing, dreaming of the spring-inspired suppers I could create with such lovely ingredients, I content myself with being a minimalist: a *crottin de Chavignol (au lait cru)* from a friendly young fellow selling at least thirty types of French cheese; some local olive tapenade from a couple who are boisterously handing out samples on little bits of baguette (I try at least five); and a petite box of fresh French framboises from a dark-haired girl whose eyes remind me of a shy doe. She offers small fraises that smell temptingly fragrant, but I've eaten a good share of fresh, organic strawberries in Carmel during the past weeks, and my weakness is always for raspberries.

Leaving the bustle of the market with a final, longing look back over my shoulder, I stroll down the hill towards the marina, where I park myself again on a sunny bench—the very same one where I sat earlier in the week, observing the festival crowds surging to and from the Palais. Seated alone, I remove the small, round cylinder of goat cheese from its paper wrapping, take the little punnet of raspberries from their bag, and proceed to tear the (somewhat diminished) baguette into chunks. Unfortunately, due to international travel on airplanes, the juniper-handled Laguiole pocketknife normally stashed at the bottom of my man-bag—always handy to have on culinary adventures—has been left at home. So I make do with breaking the disc of chèvre and mashing it with fingers into the torn hunks of bread. I contemplate opening the plastic sack of thick, inky tapenade as well, but decide that I will save it for later... and another baguette.

The combination of tangy goat cheese and fresh, rustic-style loaf is nothing short of sublime. I chew slowly, allowing the flavors to unfurl, suffusing me with a sense of well-being like a ray of sunshine. The raspberries are sweetly tart, a near perfect foil to the handcrafted bread and cheese. Warmed by the sun, surrounded by the sounds and sights of busy Cannes, watching the glittering sea reflect like diamonds, it is a meal of utmost simplicity and good taste. Food for the soul— simple, unfussy, authentic—and I feel an openness and expansion in my body as I sit, savoring the entire experience. I swear that I could eat this every day and never grow tired of it.

My body and spirit feel well fed not simply by an utterly satisfying little meal in the square by the old port, but also with my trip to the market. Indeed, beyond the bread itself, the morning has offered *le pain quotidien* for the soul. Watching the large gulls, the drifting white clouds, the noisy and colorful crowds, the expensive boats in the harbor, it all simply adds to the moment of goodness.

Wherever we may be, Soul Artists seek out true nourishment for body and soul. Just as we celebrate beauty, practice gratitude, recognize that everything is relationship, and work to expand past our limitations, it is the little soul rituals that keep us grounded in our core essence. Mindful, pleasurable experiences where senses are dilated, heart is unlatched, and the soul opens like some rare, beautiful flower. Tending to body and soul is a personal path of practice. And even when we drop or briefly lose the thread, Soul Artists always circle back to the path that leads us on towards finding our gift(s) and offering to the world.

Certainly one needn't travel to France to find beautiful food. Or to savor a simple moment of soul nourishing delight. Beauty is everywhere. In every minute, the Soul of the World reaches out, inviting us to notice, admire, celebrate and commune with it. Are we paying attention? Listening? Gentle reader, wherever you are, here's hoping that you'll enjoy *le pain quotidien* of a different sort—your daily bread for the soul, and let a sense of well-being fill you.

I wonder, how will you choose to nourish yourself today, and for what will you be most grateful?

❧ ❧ ❧

A Fine Tool in the Hand

(November, 2014)

It was billed as the World's Most Special Corkscrew.

On Christmas Eve, 1999, Paris was rocked by the storm of the century, a maestro of a tempest that ripped up roof tiles, storefront awnings, toppled trees, and wreaked havoc throughout the city and beyond. A week or so prior, on a school term break from my studies at Le Cordon Bleu, I had departed France and returned home to Hawaii. I recall sitting in our small oceanfront condo in Kona, watching and listening to the azure waves on a sunny Christmas morning, my partner browsing the news on the Internet and then suddenly exclaiming, "Wow, Paris has been destroyed! Good thing you're here and not *there*."

I returned to Paris for New Year's Eve of the millennium and discovered that the city was still recovering from the damage, and the French government had commandeered work forces from private jobs to help with the effort. When I enquired about the storm, enquiring of the woman in whose Latin Quarter flat I was staying for the school year, Roberta shrugged. "We slept through it. I woke up once, thinking there was a lot of noise outside but figured it was just revelers in the streets or some party. But when I walked outside in the morning, *oh la la! Quel désastre!*"

In addition to the widespread demolition across the city, the gale winds had wrecked a large portion of the roof at the palace of Versailles, just outside of Paris. While the historic roof was ultimately replaced, in the famous gardens the damage to many trees was sadly catastrophic, with several of the oldest toppled in the torrential winds. Among the notable casualties was the great yew tree that stood in the Queen's Grove, a nobly presiding evergreen rooted there since the days of Marie Antoinette.

Just five weeks prior to the storm, on a rare weekend outing from the rigors of culinary school, happy to escape heat of the kitchen and the grey confines of the city, I went to Versailles. Bundled up with a scarf beneath a leaden sky, I found strolling through the iconic gardens in the cool autumnal air to be more enjoyable than the palace itself. Dreaming of warm roasted chestnuts, I had ambled through the Queen's grove and certainly passed the fated yew, never guessing its final days loomed near.

After departing France in 2000, I was casually thumbing through some kitchenware catalog, as I recall, and happened across the advertisement for "The World's Most Special Corkscrew." Laguiole knives and corkscrews are known for their distinctive, gracefully curved handle and the signature Napoleonic bee affixed to the blade, each piece handmade by a single artisan. The authentic ones are engraved with the name of the forge (located in or near the village of Laguiole), distinguishing them from the abundance of cheap, mass produced knock-offs that exist.

In an effort to raise money for the post-storm restoration of the palace and gardens at Versailles, the wood from a few of the venerable, fallen trees was sold to businesses and artists for crafting into special items. And so it was that Château Laguiole, a maker of the iconic corkscrews and knives, purchased some portion of Marie Antoinette's fallen yew to fashion into handles for a limited edition piece.

When I saw the offer for the corkscrew made from the 200+ year old tree, well, I was overcome with a very rare case of "have to have it." To hell with the price. (Figure a dollar for each year the tree lived and you are pretty much on the mark.) It would be a very special memento of my culinary school adventure, never mind that I had managed to dodge the great storm, and it would remind me of France each time I opened a bottle of wine. Oh so practical. Its grain-leather, custom holster was simply an added bonus.

In a couple of earlier Soul Artist Journal posts, I have written about my fondness and deep appreciation for the space of a kitchen, its light and mood, and certainly the right tools. And I have shared previously that I count about ten favorite items in my *batterie de cuisine*, each one special to me in a unique way and carrying a story. A pleasure to use and hold, they are like old friends; the yew-handled Laguiole corkscrew most certainly resides among this special, "inner circle" group.

Crazy as it may sound given its story and irreplaceable origins, I often bring this treasure with me when I travel (though as we can no longer carry such things onboard an airplane, I stash it inside a shoe or someplace relatively obscure in my checked luggage). That's how much pleasure it brings me. Not to mention that most people, even wine lovers I know, have rubbish wine openers that offer more trouble than they are worth—cheap and flimsy things with little redeeming value other than getting the cork out (if you work hard enough, have some skill or luck, or make sufficient prayers to Dionysus).

I know, it's a bottle opener, not a pet. Perhaps I'm a bit too attached but I take the aesthetic of tools seriously. (Someday I'm likely to finally write a post about my dearest fountain pen, with which I've written every post, as well as my book manuscripts.) One of the things I most appreciate about cooking and being in the kitchen is the sensory, tactile experience of making something with my hands. As I have written elsewhere:

"A good meal brings pleasure on many levels. For one kind of cook, a significant part of that delight is the assembly of the meal itself; a sensory, creative process to be savored and enjoyed right down to the weighty heft of quality pans, the ease of sharp knives, and the feel of good tools in the hand. Each thing offers its own chant of beauty among the gathering."

I've long ago replaced anything cheap or plastic in my kitchen (my entire house, for that matter) with items that feel well made, solid and durable; things that bring pleasure from their visual and kinesthetic appeal, their heft and texture in the hand. (Similarly, food should be beautiful and it deserves a good plate, linens, and the time to savor it unhurriedly at table.) I choose to leave a few chosen items out on the counter for a sense of what they contribute to the space—a roughly-hewn Thai mortar and pestle of green marble; a uniquely inlaid bamboo rolling pin; a rustic decanter for olive oil from a noted *huilerie* in France; a handcrafted ceramic bowl piled with local fruit—as an ongoing, shifting negotiation between decor and clutter, usefulness and style.

Tonight, for the first time in quite a while, I decided to open a bottle of wine. An indulgence and brief respite from my low-glycemic diet. The cool autumnal evening and the roasted duck demanded it.

Removing the corkscrew from its sturdy leather case and opening a worthwhile bottle of Oregon Pinot Noir, I once again appreciated the elegant lines and rustic appeal of the yew handle, the rippling of its grain. In a small way, a grand and noble tree lives on, still offering beauty. I savored the way it felt in my grip, praising the sharpness of the serrated blade for cutting through the ring of foil at the top of the bottle neck. Solid. Hand-crafted with pride of workmanship. As a once-beekeeper (but now too nomadic), I adore the Napoleonic bee affixed to the spine. The wood's finish has worn to a dull shine like dark honey, and my French one-of-a-kind, oh-so-practical *objet d'art* is a delight to hold and to use.

Regular readers of this journal know that I'm easily captivated by the small pleasures in the day. Those little human moments, where I'm suddenly deeply engrossed in the sensuality of the moment and how it *feels*—including what is in my hands—are simple celebrations of life. My dear fountain pen scrawling away on the pages of a notebook. The worn, French vegetable peeler as it denudes a potato. A sturdy wooden broom made with old-fashioned corn fibers as it sweeps the front porch and steps, *whsssk, whsssk*. My handmade elk hide drum. A master potter's ceramic mug, uniquely glazed, filled with a steaming, fragrant brew and cradled in cupped palms.

Soul Artists know that life is not always art but there exists an art to living. We create and appreciate simple, daily rituals to tend the soul. Writing a poem. Nurturing the garden. Cooking an appealing meal and then sitting down to enjoy it with gratitude, friendship, laughter and love. A leisurely stroll though the neighborhood or surrounding landscape, our senses ajar. And we know that little could be more important than nourishing the *bodysoul*, or quiet time for inspiration and rest. As with making a proper cup of tea, even opening a bottle of wine can be a small ritual—appreciating the tool in the hand, the wine glasses, the liquid's hue—or using any objects we've gathered in a sensual celebration of life.

As I have queried before, gentle reader, *what is the art you make of your life?* And what did you do for that art today? Here's hoping that you possess a few special objects or tools that feel like old friends, ones that deliver a tactile pleasure when using them—offering something more than mere functionality, and inviting you to mindfully appreciate the moment, even if fleeting. Beauty feeds the soul, my friend. Indeed, the simplest things are often the most beautiful.

Open your senses and celebrate.

ॐ ॐ ॐ

Cuisine of the Sun: Mediterranean Grilled Chicken
(June, 2013)

I t happened again today, twice. I was seduced by *light*.

The first occurrence was late afternoon (17:40 to be precise), when I was mesmerized by a slanting sunbeam as it illuminated the rattan weavings beneath the glass of our mahogany coffee table, causing it to glow and come nearly to life. Finished with my writing work, I was reading on the couch when suddenly I became aware of the greater moment—as if someone or something had just quietly entered the room—and lay my book aside, reveling in the luminous ambience.

The second instance was just slightly later after supper—out walking with the dogs in our new neighborhood—when I became entranced by the soft, powdery blue of the Pacific sky strewn with fluffy pink clouds. As the sun descended towards the welcoming arms of the sea, I stood enchanted, gazing up at the heavens and jagged green shards of the tropical mountains, while a soft breeze tousled my hair and rustled the nearby palm tree fronds. Two English Whippets tugged at their leads impatiently, eager to get on. *What is he looking at?!?*

When I lived in the high desert of New Mexico—long known for its remarkable quality of light, luring famous American artists like early Modernist painter Georgia O'Keeffe and photographer Ansel Adams—late afternoon was a holy time for me. I would often stop whatever I was doing so that I could go outside and marvel at the display of illumination on the Sangre de Cristo Mountains. The "golden hour" was always stunning. Magical, even. Living in Santa Fe, if I was free in the late afternoon, I liked to go to a little tea house in an old adobe at the upper end of Canyon Road (a mile-long stretch of expensive galleries and *ateliers*), where I would sit on the patio with a cup of *chai* and savor the vividly painted moment as it enveloped my world.

The intensely captivating light show lasted only a few fleeting minutes, gracing each thing it touched as if somehow illumined from within. *El fuego sagrado del Díos*, I used to call it—the sacred fire of God.

I should have been a painter, I suppose. I've often thought it would be far preferable to have an unfinished work on canvas at the end of the day rather than orderly rows of tangled sentences, a jumble of half-polished words on a screen or paper. A painting seems far more tangible somehow. And yet I likely would have despaired at never being able to even come close to capturing with pigments the elusive quality of illumination that opens all my senses and stirs my soul. Instead, I simply lose myself in moments of light, feeling my heart flutter in my chest as if it had wings.

Rather than with an artist's brush, I often chase fleeting moments of sensory inspiration through cooking. Perhaps they are not so different, painting and cooking (although one tastes decidedly better). Certainly, both can be creative, and good meals invoke a sensory revelation. Moreover, some food seems to celebrate the light itself.

It's summer in the Northern Hemisphere and I wish to take you somewhere—someplace that words cannot adequately go. I want to give you a polysensory experience, with taste leading the way. I'm going to offer you a recipe for a simple meal, the kind that should be eaten outdoors. In the right frame of mind, the bright interplay of flavors can transport you to a shaded arbor of rustling grapevines somewhere near the shore, watching the play of sunlight and shadows on arid foothills and a flashing turquoise sea. This is rustic, unadorned food that speaks of bold, summer days as it feeds your soul.

Living on the Mediterranean is where I discovered that the taste of garlicky yogurt and olive oil is, well, addictive. For the ultimate mélange of flavors, the chicken should be grilled; there's something incomparable that the element of fire adds to food. (If we were living in the Old World, we might be lucky enough to cook this in a wood-burning oven, very close to heaven.) Lacking a grill (or whichever sort), you can also pan sear it—the taste will still be delicious. If you don't eat chicken or meat, you could substitute a variety of summer vegetables to grill instead. Brush them lightly with a good olive oil, sprinkle with sea salt and freshly ground pepper, and grill until lightly charred on both sides.

I confess that I'm not one to follow recipes exactly. Far from it. Mostly I cook by feel and intuition. When I do need measurements, my choice is always to use metric as I find it a superior and easier system (you can take the man out of Europe but...). The entire world uses metric except us Americans. <sigh> Here I give both metric and imperial measurements for convenience, but please take the amounts as merely guidelines and adapt as you deem appropriate.

If you can get organic ingredients and a free-range, non-frozen chicken, use them.

ɛෆ

Grilled Chicken with Yogurt Sauce

Ingredients:

4 chicken breasts, skin on (preferably free-range and unfrozen)
1–2 teaspoons good quality sea salt, preferably coarse (see note below *)
juice of 1 lemon
½–1 teaspoon red chile flakes
1–2 teaspoons finely diced fresh rosemary (optional)
freshly ground black pepper
3 tablespoons extra virgin olive oil

Yogurt Sauce:

1 cup (240 ml) thick Greek-style yogurt, plain
2 garlic cloves, peeled and smashed
good pinch of sea salt
¼ cup (60 ml) extra virgin olive oil (or more to taste)
juice of half a lemon

As accompaniment:

three large handfuls of wild or baby arugula ("rocket," roquette, etc.) or other small, garden fresh lettuce
a dozen ripe cherry tomatoes, halved
¼ cup (40g) toasted pumpkin seeds

ဢ

*Cook's note: First, salt—good salt—is not the enemy as it has been made to be in America. A quality sea salt is rich in minerals and trace elements needed by our body, and has a far more complex taste than the conventional table salt (which is simply sodium chloride with anti-caking elements added so that it will pour easily). If there's a single, easy thing to do to immediately improve the flavor of your cooking, toss that container of Morton's in the rubbish bin and get some quality sea salt. Though it is expensive, almost exclusively I use Maldon, an exquisite, flaky salt from Essex, England. I'm also fond of grey Celtic sea salt from Brittany, France,

and *fleur de sel* ("flower of salt"). Lighter, coarse, flaky salts (including kosher) are actually less "salty" than standard salt, and more can (should) be used in salting and brining. Cooks and chefs will debate this endlessly, both claiming science on their side, but in my experience salting meat or poultry early helps draw out the flavor whilst cooking and improves its taste and texture on subtle levels; whereas salting late or at the end of cooking generally just makes food taste salty.

Method:

At least three hours ahead of cooking, generously season the chicken breasts with sea salt (alternatively, brine them, if you're knowledgeable about that technique). Let them rest in the fridge until about an hour before cooking, then bring to room temperature.

Brush off any excess salt. Sprinkle with the lemon juice and chile flakes (and rosemary, if using), along with some grindings of black pepper. Drizzle with a bit of olive oil and massage it into the flesh.

For the sauce: put the yogurt into a small bowl and add the garlic, salt, olive oil and lemon. Mix well and allow it to sit for at least an hour at room temperature, giving an occasional stir to move the crushed garlic through the sauce and better infuse its flavor. Taste and adjust the seasoning as necessary, adding more olive oil if you prefer. (Note: a pinch of spice would not be out of place here—red chile, *pimentón ahumado* (smoked paprika), ground chipotle, *ras al hanout* (Moroccan seasoning), Turkish chile flakes such as *marash* or *urfa* chiles—but the sauce also stands well on its own). Remove the garlic before serving.

Using a cast iron or heavy-weight pan, toast the pumpkin seeds over medium heat until golden and beginning to pop, shaking the pan often to keep them from burning. Remove from the hot pan (otherwise they'll continue to cook and burn), sprinkle lightly with salt, and allow to cool. Set aside.

Preheat the grill. When hot, lay the chicken breasts skin-side down on the rack and cook for 5–8 minutes. Then turn and grill the other side. (Total cooking time will depend on your grill, whether using coals or propane, and the level of heat). The skin should be pleasantly charred in some places, with the flesh underneath still juicy and meltingly tender.

For the accompanying greens, you can either serve them plain, using the sauce as a dressing, or lightly dress with a simple vinaigrette. Top with the sliced cherry tomatoes and toasted pumpkin seeds. Serve the chicken alongside and spoon the yogurt sauce over.

℘

Finally...

If you're a wine drinker, transport yourself to the Mediterranean and enjoy this with a pale, salmon-colored, dry Provençal rosé (Domaine Tempier is a nice, if pricey, choice) or a richer Tavel (from the southern Rhône region). Forget everything you think you know about rosé wine (which in the States is only just emerging, two decades later, from the influence of innocuous, mass produced, sweet pink wines like White Zinfandel). Summer is here... drink pink! Alternatively, serve a tall pitcher of fresh, organic lemonade made with sparkling water, infused with sprigs of fresh mint.

Now, take the plates outdoors where you can sit in the shade and dine *al fresco,* relishing the contrasts and complements of flavors in the summer light. Let yourself be seduced by a feast for the senses. Eat as a Soul Artist: dining slowly, opening to the 'other-than-human' world around you, savoring the moment. Share this rustic fare with good friends or someone you love, basking in the *joie de vivre* of the passing day and appreciating the gift of being alive.

Often it is the simplest things that are the most beautiful, rewarding, and special, especially when we celebrate them as nourishment for body and soul.

❧ ❧ ❧

Hummingbirds and Communion

(August, 2014)

The little jeweled acrobat zoomed up to the window, hovered for a moment as if peering at me, then shot straight upward and disappeared from sight.

I arrived back at my friends' welcoming sanctuary of a house, a place that has become a home away from home, and one of my favorite oases. This trip, I am scouting nearby for a *pied à terre*, a modest writer's retreat, a little haven of my own (at least to rent) where I might escape from Hawaii, and it looks like I may have found the golden ticket. Fingers crossed. In the meantime, I am resting and taking things easy. Walking the parched, brown land in the valley (or occasionally the sea shore), my unsheathed soles on the bare soil or pale sand, senses and heart open wide. I am shifting, listening, harmonizing, and coming back into resonance with this landscape and place—a *soulscape*—where I am at home in my own skin, once again fully myself, both domestic and wild.

Dwell in possibility, I remind myself, fingering the bodhi seed *mala* that perpetually adorns my left wrist.

Here, I am watching the diverse array of birds and the shy, black-tailed mule deer in the shade of the oaks. Washing dishes and pouring the conserved water onto the thirsty garden plants, as my hosts prefer. Yesterday I sat near the bee hives, observing those little winged alchemists come and go like darting golden missiles of love. Cooking fresh, flavorful meals for my friends and then savoring them with good wine and deep conversation, a sharing that ranges from soul poetry to shamanism to shadow work. It is a soul nourishing time and place, and I am hungry for it.

Seated at the rectangular dining table, a steaming cup of robust tea beside me, I smiled. I have adored hummingbirds for as long as I can recall appreciating *any* wild thing, and they continue to infuse my spirit with a sense of effervescent joy whenever they dart near.

These amazing, delicate birds were beloved by my mother, and I remember the day as a young man when they became inextricably linked with her in my mind. It was early February, just a few days before Valentine's Day, and my mom lay in a hospice bed in a downstairs room of our South Pasadena home, preparing to transit from this world. The home health aide and a few, immediate family members were gathered bedside, and I sat holding her pale, frail hand, watching her shallow breathing, knowing the moment had come for her to depart. Heeding some prompt, I looked up and saw a hummingbird hovering right outside the French doors, beneath the arbor of fuchsia-colored bougainvillea, as if it was looking in. Just a few breaths later, my mother's spirit slipped quietly away with a final, soft whisper.

As I stood outdoors on the rear lawn and wept hot, salty tears, a hummingbird flew up to me and hovered right near my head for several moments. Then it rocketed away. Such a thing had never happened to me before, and in my bereavement I felt it was somehow a sign from my mother—that she was finally free and yet still with me.

After the funeral, one of the things I chose from her belongings was a delicate wooden carving of a hummingbird feeding its two young in a nest. The adult is a separate piece; the long, narrow vertical bill, when inserted into one of the open-beaked juveniles, carefully balances the parent overhead with wings spread. Perhaps five-inches high, this little handcrafted wonder was brought from Japan by my grandparents as a gift to my mother, and I long fancied it, even before it came to be mine. In my years of roaming and moving house, I have boxed up the miniature sculpture protectively and carried it along as a treasure. Usually it rests upon my altar of precious things, its base nestled within a small, immaculately woven bird nest I found at our house when we dwelt on the Big Island of Hawai'i.

Throughout my early and mid-adulthood, whenever a hummingbird appeared, I thought of my mother and felt an immediate sense of warm joy and delight. Both times that I resided in New Mexico, from late spring until the autumn, they seemed to be everywhere about, peppering the air, some fifteen species (or more) having returned from their wintering in Mexico and further south. *Zoom, zoom, zoom,* they filled my soul with bright sparkles whether I was indoors or out, for the thrum of their wings is loud enough to be heard through the open windows, zipping around on the sage-scented breeze.

Living in Europe where hummingbirds do not exist, I often missed their brilliantly iridescent, acrobatic presence. These miraculous tiny birds, who can hover in place (or even fly backwards) with wings that beat between 50 and 200 times *per second,* somehow seem to carry the energy of joy. Like honeybees, they inspire me. For many years, above my small writing desk, pinned to the cork board amid other chosen mementos, pictures, and inspirational quotes, I kept a handcrafted card of an emerald-breasted male "hummer" with the words at the bottom of the photo, *What would you do if you knew you could not fail?*

Disappointingly for me, hummingbirds do not live in Hawaii, where I currently reside, and their introduction to the islands is forbidden by law. Did you know that the natural pollinator of the pineapple is this amazing little bird? Or that when pineapples are pollinated, the fruit produces seeds? An undesirable trait (particularly for the pineapple industry).

On my increasingly frequent visits to the central California coast, staying at my friends' home in rural Carmel Valley, I have delighted in the sonic, vivid presence of these birds in the garden and all around, surprised to find a few of them here even in the winter (the majority migrate south to warmer climes). Yesterday in the late afternoon, as the day faded toward its golden hour, five Anna's hummingbirds (the most common variety) zoomed around the rear deck of the house, noisily chasing each other. I stopped my prep work in the kitchen and stood by the glass doors to watch their antics, an elated inner child very close to the surface and a smile on my face. Wondrous.

This morning, as the lone hummer hovers briefly outside the dining room windows, beside me on the table sits one of the books I am currently reading: a collection of poems by Carolyn Brigit Flynn titled, *Communion: In Praise of the Sacred Earth* (White Cloud Press, 2014). The cover bears a beautiful photograph of a female hummingbird with her shawl of iridescent green feathers feeding from some small, pink flowers.

A hummingbird at the window, and one on the table.

Flynn's offering of devotional poetry is remarkable, ranging from deeply reverent and celebratory to heart-rending; I am nearly as smitten with it as I am with those little jeweled acrobats themselves. I wrote to the author, "Receiving this beautiful book is like someone placed a treasure in my outstretched hands." I have been reading her poems aloud, one each morning, as I step outdoors to greet the day in my barefoot manner, each one an offering to the Holy. More than a couple have been earmarked for my newly established soul practice of learning poems by heart, inspired by recently attending the Redwoods Men's Conference. As Bill, a poet there says, "There can never be enough spoken poetry. Each poem spoken aloud restores soul to the world." I'll drink to that.

Ms. Flynn, with whom I am having a private, one-on-one lunch tomorrow in Santa Cruz (we have the same publisher), describes how the poems came to be. From her book's Preface:

> "*For over a year, I woke at dawn and came to my writing table set before a wide sliding-glass window. I greeted the sky, three redwood trees across the way, the tall birch in our garden, and mourning doves, crows, squirrels, ring-necked pigeons and robins there on any given day. Then I opened The Book of Hours by Rainer Maria Rilke. Each morning I read one poem, and found myself in a call and response, writing a new poem with one of Rilke's lines as the title...*
>
> *... I found myself spontaneously addressing the sacred presence of the earth directly, as 'Beloved.' In that moment the divine essence, often called God as well as many other names in the world's spiritual traditions, became for me an intimate beloved, the embodied earth herself, living daily with us, within and among the trees, creatures, stones, flowers, and within ourselves.*"

So much soul-stirring beauty abounds in this slim volume of a book, it seems quite appropriate to have a hummingbird on its cover.

To that end, Carolyn Brigit Flynn's gem in hand, here is the poem that yesterday I took into my bones and breath, adding it to the others that I carry within my heart:

"Only With Our Doing Can We Grasp You"

I will take you in my hands
today, Beloved, and love you
as you grow in the ground.
I will touch your soft fur,
and your warm lover's skin
in the morning sheets.

In the afternoon,
I will sit within you
as light floods the garden.
And the bees, loving the flowers,
will be praised by my eyes.

If I could stitch the world together
with my loving, as do the bees,
I would, my Beloved, I would.
I would live like this:
as though my every touch
kept the world alive,
knitted together in this graceful hum.
  ~ Carolyn Brigit Flynn

Coastal clouds which earlier obscured the brown, oak-studded hills have traveled on, and the day outside shines bright, sunny, and warm. A hummingbird—the same one from earlier?—flies like a meteor past the windows with an audible *thrum*. The bees are dancing among the plants and flowers of the deck, loving them. I am called to go outside and sit, to breathe, to savor the moment and the beauty that enfolds.

Soul Artists know that life is at its largest, most powerful, and most content when we are actively engaged in a meaningful conversation with the many realms. In our work, our play, in our living and loving and losing, these are the passages and transitions of transformation. Soul, our creative essence, longs for an authentic exchange with the 'more-than-human' world. When we cast our senses and heart wide to what surrounds, when we respond to the summons of the places and passions that call to us, we initiate that deep, often wordless communication. Or communion. We enter into intimate relationship with the Larger Story, and we must offer something of value in return.

Gentle reader, here's hoping that you engage in your own sense of communion today. Every day. Whether inspired by the small bird at your window, the rustle of wind in the green silver trees, the ribbons of light arcing across the sky, or some other moment of beauty that reaches out and touches you, may your soul open a bit wider in gratitude. Even in our struggles, beauty and grace surround us. As I so frequently ask, *to what will you give the gift of your attention?*

Put another way, what waits to be noticed—held in the gaze of an undefended heart—and recognized in a moment of silent, energetic communion?

❧ ❧ ❧

Writing the Soul: An Ongoing Journey
(April, 2016)

I t's a fine feeling to finish writing a book.

There is a tremendous sense of accomplishment, of having succeeded at a daunting task like climbing a mountain. On the body level, one feels an openness of the heart, belly and breath, and if we have dared to tell the truth, a resonance in the bones like soft thunder.

Finish may be a somewhat loose word, for there is always more work that could be done on a thing, another rise to climb in order to actually gain the summit—and that's before the long hurry-up-and-wait of the actual publishing process and the book going to print. But last week I completed the first major edit of my most recent work, the preliminary combing through of a manuscript I wrote last spring when I returned from France.

It was something of a torrent. Seated at the small table by the window, nearly a hundred thousand words poured from my trusty pen in a mere three weeks, filling two French notebooks (preferred for their silky paper) with jumbled script. Busy at the time with the ongoing work of building an author's platform and promoting *The Bones & Breath*, I then essentially set the freshly written work aside for six months, typing in bits and pieces at a time, a chapter here and there. It wasn't until January that I took it up again in earnest, a proverbial chisel and mallet in my hand, and began chipping away at the stack of printed pages sitting in my carved wooden writer's box.

Having been down this road before with *Bones,* I know that there are more edits needed on the manuscript. I face another round of polishing and smoothing before I offer it to select early readers, and then after weighing their comments and suggestions, another comb through—minimum—before I embark on the quest of finding a publisher and querying agents. [insert heavy sigh here] At the moment, however, I am savoring a feeling of sweetness and accomplishment. The hardest part of the climb is over, and from the ridge top I can see the glimmering sea stretching to the far line of the horizon. It's a damn fine view.

It was just before lunch when I reached the last sentence of the final page (and changed it), and laying aside my dear old fountain pen, pushed back the chair, and smiled. Then I stood and walked around the silence of this rented coastal cottage, gazing out the thin, filmy windows at the blustery spring day, observing the limbs of the Grandmother Monterey cypress swaying and waving in the wind as if in celebration. I nearly floated with a lightness of being, and the gentle effervescence bubbling up in my core simply added to my grin.

The irony is that I never intended to write this book. I had fully planned that my second published offering would be the follow-up to *The Bones & Breath*. Essentially the remainder of the original manuscript that I cut in half to make that first book, the work sits in my desk drawer, waiting patiently for its time in the sun. Instead, this new manuscript manifested after I met Marlena de Blasi, internationally-bestselling author of *A Thousand Days in Venice*, and *A Thousand Days in Tuscany*, a million-to-one chance last May at a Left Bank café in Paris. [Read "A Paris Encounter: Meeting de Blasi"]

The overall tale is too long for this post, so suffice it to say that had our paths not crossed, meeting the woman whose gilded memoirs I adored and savored whilst residing in England, I would never have considered writing my own story about living abroad. There are other mysterious currents besides the Marlena factor, however, for had my initial book been any sort of commercial success, or had doors opened as I anticipated, I would simply have proceeded with the follow-up in the desk drawer. And this new, very personal work would be nothing but colored sparks of memories flashing like meteors though my mind. Funny, that.

I am still toying with the subtitle (which a publisher can change anyway), but "Fields, Foxes and Tea" is decidedly something more than a travelogue about two Americans living in soggy old England. It is a story about second chances, being an outsider, finding our true work in the world, the power of nature, and what nourishes the soul. The French-trained cook in me has insisted that there are abundant servings of good food, and all of the tale is touched with a bit of Old World magic.

During the writing and subsequent editing, I wrestled at moments with how much to bring forward and share, both in regards to details of our personal life, as well as my own beliefs about the nature of things—hidden and apparent. The work of words aside, isn't that really how it is for each of us, every day, deciding how fully we reveal our deepest, most authentic self?

The core of my offering in the world, both with healing arts/coaching clients and writing, centers on authenticity and expansion. *Risk it all*, I decided at moments of indecision. I already took off all my clothes and walked naked across a Kentish field in the opening of my first book, so what do I have to hide? (Several readers have enquired whether I *really* did that or whether it was just some type of metaphor; when I assure them it was nakedly true, they are either incredulous or secretly envious, perhaps a bit of both.)

Sometimes, often in fact, the path at our feet doesn't lead where we thought it was headed, and it might even take us in an entirely different direction than what we had planned for ourselves. Fate moves in mysterious ways. The relevant query, regardless of where the track seems to be leading, is whether it has heart and soul. Does it instill openness in the chest and belly when we consider it—even if we're unsure or afraid we cannot really accomplish this thing we're debating, the thread we are following…?

Trust the *bodysoul* and heart, not the monkey mind or the caller of fears. Believe that something in your core, the deepest and most creatively authentic aspect of you—along with the Mystery—knows where you most need to go, guiding through strange fate and curious events. And though much to the ego's resistance and dismay, our real job—at least if we wish to awaken to a larger life—is to let go the illusion of safety, following our allurement and intuition, even at the risk of being cracked open or failing. Yes, especially then. For as I said in last week's post, only when the shell has broken can we emerge to something much larger.

Back in January 2014, I wrote a post titled "In the Realm of Falcons" recounting a New Year's Day hike in Big Sur that proved far more difficult and led me much higher and further than I anticipated.

Soul projects are often like that rigorous climb. A hundred times during the ascent you might swear to yourself that you'll *never* do this again. There are moments when you think you've reached the top, only to discover with a sinking heart (and perhaps a tired, delirious laugh) that there's another rise beyond, and apparently one more after that.

But eventually, you *do* reach the summit, limbs trembling and exhausted, and look out over the world, weak but elated, the sea shining with diamond light far below you. How very far you have come.

Could anything be more important than being deeply, fully authentic to your soul? Not really.

Friend, whether it's a book dreaming inside you or something else entirely, here's hoping that you'll heed the nudge in that direction and embark upon an uncharted journey. May you find the willingness and courage not only to begin and remain true to yourself—to risk it all—but to keep going when the path grows unexpectedly steep and you are trudging uphill, one foot after the other. And whether it is a falcon or an angel (human or otherwise) that mysteriously appears to inspire you to trudge on, or simply your own dogged self-determination and refusal to quit, may you reach the true summit and then look back, deeply glad that you came this way.

Onward to the next book.

❧ ❧ ❧

Spirits of Cedar: A Walk on the Mountain
(February, 2013)

Days of monsoon-like rain. Nights of howling wind and crashing trees. A brown torrent courses along the driveway, washing away all the gravel and anything in its path. The ravine below our house, which normally sits dry, is a raging current alive with voices as water hurls down the mountain. A bit lower on the slopes, a house was swept off its foundation into a gulch.

After too many days indoors and nearly a week of storms, finally, a sunny morning invites me out for a wander. I've donned my battered, wide-brimmed walking hat, not just because it's part of my outdoors attire but also due to the light mist that continues to fall despite a blue sky. Lazy, inelastic muscles are eager to be stretched, and my heart longs for the pump of exercise and animating breath. Heading out from the house and up the hill, my tight hips and knees feel like creaky doors too long unopened.

Two days ago in the tempest, a great salt cedar toppled at the head of our road, falling across the neighbor's drive and smashing his fence and gate, effectively leaving him trapped. I pause for a while, considering the impressive tree and its uprooted fate, feeling a twinge of blue sadness that such a noble giant stands no more. It was a beautiful tree, sculpted by a lifetime of winds into a graceful, windswept poem as skillfully as if an artist's watercolor brush had trailed it eloquently across an open page. The collective work of a couple of chainsaws has restored access to the road, and the venerable cedar is now a jumble of cut logs that smell fragrantly. Standing there, I feel an impulse to lightly run my hands over the great cut limbs, feeling for life in the wet wood as I offer last rites and soft words of appreciation, and then touching scented fingertips to my face and lips.

Holy, holy...

As I walk on, the tarmac still glistens with water as if I am treading on shiny obsidian glass that doesn't crack. Much of the road is in a poor state, piled with gravel and mud washed down in impressive amounts. Just a bit further along, a narrow bridge spans the gulch and I can hear the loud voices of water as I approach. Yesterday, despite the depth of the ravine and the large drainpipe under road, so great a volume roared down the mountain that the deluge was over the road, making it impassable except with four-wheel drive. The rushing water is lower today but the normally dry gully is a series of cascading waterfalls and swirling, muddy pools. It's an impressive, captivating sight and I linger, listening to the new chorus of high and low notes in a liquid choir, drinking all in through open senses.

Passing the junkyard house at the top of Pi'iholo Road, a resident flock of feral chickens that seems to always be strutting and dandying about the road, squawks and disbands at my approach, alerted by the golden and ruby cockerel's bossy warnings, scattering off into the thickets of wild white ginger.

Just around the corner, I reach the Forest Reserve and its wide, metal gate, where there is a trail I normally tread barefoot several days a week. Here is where I come for my *earthing* time, my grounding meditation and sensory communion. Passing the portal, there is a somatic upwelling in my body, a steady streaming of energy like a subterranean spring pushing forth.

Shed your shoes.

It's a command, not an option. I hesitate for a moment as I contemplate the muddiness of the earth but then step free of my well-worn walking sandals. Wide, bare feet sink just slightly into the soggy, cool red soil and I feel myself involuntarily inhale a deep breath.

Yes... good.

As I begin my barefoot wander along the track, I marvel at how the forces of water have rearranged the scene. The usual, half-foot deep carpet of pine needles is entirely absent, swept away somewhere, and the trail is a rusty snake studded with grey stones. The sensation through my soles anchors me firmly in bodysoul, a tender and vivid exchange with every step.

Shortly into the ramble, I hop cross a clear stream (which doesn't normally exist), awed by the jumble of fallen trees and tangle of destruction deposited in the storm's wake. It's apparent that a considerable wall of water hurtled down this gentle fold. Everywhere, the landscape is familiar but rearranged; oddly mirroring my own life, I muse, given the extended stay of mother-in-law and my partner's young, startlingly immature cousin. *Microcosm mirrors macrocosm.* The storm on the mountain, however disruptive, is merely a passing moment in the cyclical rhythms of nature; a squall that will pass, whether through the forest or my living room. Just some weather. A wee bit of drama in a small saga while the Larger Story goes on, unperturbed.

Amidst the trees my mood has improved immeasurably, as it always does. I've come home to myself, once again cognizant of the larger, mythic frame. Slowly I meander the forest trail loop, my Keen outdoor sandals dangling in hand, soles (and soul) softly squishing in wet, muddy earth... offering quiet, heartfelt blessings with each step.

At one point, I pause again to commune more deeply with the mountain forest around me. Using both a visual and feeling sense, I "touch in" with the trees. Feeling. Listening. Connecting with the invisibles—a world of energy, subtle perceptions, and emotion—this style of sensing or knowing is both underdeveloped and under-appreciated in Western cultures. Yet we all do this on a certain level, as when we step into an unfamiliar room full of people and quickly sweep it over with some invisible sense, detecting how it feels—whether it is safe, inviting, or bristling with unfriendly eyes.

The living intelligence and creativity of the Cosmos permeates everything from atoms to cedar trees to supernovas. Indeed, we dwell in a fully participatory and reciprocally sensing Universe; we cannot perceive a thing without it also perceiving us. Despite claims of scientists and researchers (or anyone, really), there is no such thing as a truly objective experience, as demonstrated even on the quantum level. What we observe, touch, or interact with will respond, react, or touch *us* in return.

In this form of sensing, of reaching out, there exists a moment when both beings experience something of the other. It's a feeling for which there is no word in our impoverished English language. The Athenians called it *aisthesis*: the experience of perceiving the touch of life, of a particular kind of 'other-than-human' awareness on us, in reciprocity. For the ancient Greeks, the organ of aisthesis was the heart, that part of us that is capable of feeling. Further, it was understood that this exchange, this non-physical touch between the human and non-human world, opens moments of perception and understanding when insights flow into us that can arrive no other way.

Where we most powerfully recognize this sort of exchange is in the living realm of Nature. Reaching out and touching the wildness of the world and Nature's soul, something new—and essential—arrives in us. As with the breath, we open in inspiration. Indeed, if we observe our bodymind in this mutual "touching" or sensing, in addition to the affect or feeling, there is also a simultaneous change of physiology. A somatic response ensues: a dilation of the heart's energetic field, a deepening of breath, a relaxation or settling.

I *feel* into the forest, noting what I perceive in my body, trying on different words to find the right fit. *Renewal* comes close. The mood feels harmonious, even if still adjusting to the new arrangement of things after significant motion. In my very expansive, sensing state, I also detect a soft upwelling in each living thing, a surge upwards towards the heavens. Further reaching out and sensing more keenly, I feel each of these new qualities in my own bodysoul—a somatic communion. By "tuning in" on a feeling level to the living world around me, my mood and physiology have shifted.

In this reciprocal sensing, I wonder what the forest feels in *me...*?

Mindfully walking the return aspect of the trail loop, in a gentle reverie, my attention is drawn by the unusual sounds of a tree I am passing. I'm well acquainted with the usual clacking of branches in the winds here on the mountain, even the way that the various voices take on almost human qualities. (The ancient Hawaiians considered these upper forests to be the realm of spirits.) This sound is different: a low base note, it's not unlike a cello's strings. I halt and look up into the tree, scanning the limbs that must somehow be rubbing against another to create an almost musical noise.

From a cedar directly in front of me, just above my head, a branch as thick as two human arms emerges from its great trunk and rubs against another cedar several feet away. For so long has the limb massaged and stroked its neighbor that a smooth, shiny groove has been rubbed into the other's trunk. Meanwhile, the neighbor has continued to grow and expand its diameter, thus the newer growth has formed a cusp around the sliding branch. Like a pair of cupped hands, the worn slot holds and encloses the other's appendage as it moves; a sufficiently deep C-shape that the rubbing branch cannot escape or be freed from the surrounding groove. It can only side back and forth as the two trees sway in the wind, jointly creating sounds and music of deep, low reverberations.

I stand there for a full five minutes, marveling at this unique arrangement while absorbing the sounds—feeling the resonance in my own body. How long has it taken for such an enclosing grasp to form in hard cedar wood? Unguessed at years, through which these two beings have stood side by side in relationship, making music together.

To the tuned-out, disaffected juvenile staying in our house, at dinner I repeatedly pose the question, "What was the most interesting thing that you observed today?" Marveling at the cello trees, as I think of them now, my own answer is delightfully clear.

I finally amble on to the end of the trail where, at the gate, I turn and offer a ritual bow of acknowledgment and gratitude to the mountain wood. Then I fasten the battered Keen sandals onto my muddy feet for the mile and a half distance to our cottage. Walking through sunlight and lightly swirling mists, listening to the voices of wind and trees, I savor the profound lightness in my body, so profoundly different from when I set out on this walk just an hour ago.
Returning past the fallen, dismembered evergreen at the top of our road, its notes of freshly sawn cedar hitting my nostrils, I again feel currents of soft, blue grief inside; a sadness that I will no more hear the wind spirits sighing and speaking through its great boughs when I pass by.

I am nearly at our driveway when a curious memory arrives, as if a little bird has alighted and carried a thought in its beak to drop into my head. I recall two men we met while living in southern Spain, where we hoped to build a new life in the rugged mountains of Andalucía amid the silvery olive groves. They were a delightful couple in their early forties, one English and one American, hard at work renovating and reopening an impressive bed and breakfast in a 300-year old farmhouse. One of them had recently left the cutthroat corporate world of London because, as he put it, he had wearied of sitting in meetings where daily he had to provide a suitable answer to the question, "What did you do today to justify your existence [at this company]?"

As this memory pops unbidden into my consciousness, for a moment I consider that we each might do well to pose a similar but gentler question to ourselves: *What did you do today to celebrate your existence as a human soul?*

If you ask me today, my answer is simple: I walked barefoot on the earth. I opened my senses and marveled.

Or simpler yet:

I felt... deeply.

❧ ❧ ❧

Roots for the Soul
(May, 2016)

The black plastic pots of lavender and rosemary on the front deck need a permanent home. So do I.

As I watered and tended them, still fussing over the collateral damage incurred last week during the great Monterey cypress cutting [read "Saving the Grandmother"], I lamented that they were not yet in the ground and nicely settled. That said, they likely would have suffered far more injury were they planted—witness the ornamental plum whose entire top was roughly shorn by a falling, amputated limb of the tree—because I was able to move them under the sheltering eaves of the roof.

Previously I wrote in a post that if you visited this little cottage where I currently reside, but for the single orchid at the kitchen sink and these potted lovelies on the deck, you wouldn't likely guess that I'm a plant lover. The same could be said for books, or the relative scarcity of them in this house. This situation is largely because I have been a nomad for too long, and I grew tired of giving away my leafy green children each time the painted gypsy caravan rolled on to its new campsite (or sailed across an ocean, always very difficult for plants).

And so I have only these few select companions, along with two cherry tomato starts that were recently given to me. There is always lavender growing just outside my house, whether I've planted it there or not; it seems to be part and parcel of who I am, and I adore its narrow, silver green leaves and spikes of fragrant, purple beauty. It's a profoundly healing plant, lavender, and I guess I would go so far as to consider it a "plant ally" of sorts. Some people have "totem animals," others have plants. Some of us have both.

Rosemary too, or *romarin*, as I like to call it, as if we were both thriving in sunny, arid Provence. Another powerfully medicinal plant, it's a healer's friend—to say nothing of being a constant companion in the kitchen, finding its way into this dish and that. Cookies, even. This one too, like lavender, I need close at hand where I can rub my hands over it each time I pass and then lift palms to my face, inhaling the resinous goodness.

Initially these plant friends of mine remained in their somewhat ugly containers on the front deck because it receives the only significant sunshine in the front garden, given the shade of the grandmother Monterey cypress. That's what I reasoned, anyway. The other facet of truth is that I'm always moving on, and I had only selected this cottage as a temporary landing spot, one that I didn't plan to be at more than a year—and I'm not leaving any more green companions behind.

Be ready for travel, is essentially what I've told them.

I have spent the entire month of April with my arse essentially parked in my desk chair, spending eight hours each day diligently editing the recently completed manuscript for a memoir about our years of living in England. Wading through that process, trusty fountain pen in hand, I am saliently clear of the profound longing for a place to call home weaving through this story of our ongoing travels. I feel it even now, a swirling blue spiral in my chest around the heart. Wistful.

More than once in this journal I have lamented how weary I am of the nomadic life, wishing only for the place that both my beloved and I feel called to put down roots, where we feel the nurturing of nature and culture, where we might park the painted gypsy wagon to let the wheels rot off beneath a grand old tree. A home where I can finally start a proper vegetable patch, because I don't need the landlord's permission and I'm not moving on, and these dear little green ones can find their place in the earth and remain as the seasons roll by.

Ours is a rootless and alienated culture overall. Lacking real ties to the land where we dwell and severed from a sense of relationship with place, like tumbleweeds we ceaselessly roll on to the next destination, job, or passing fad. It's almost like an inability to maintain a long-term relationship, thinking there must be someone prettier and more alluring, less difficult to live with, or generally better suited to us. We think we have freedom in our mobility, but mostly I think we are suffering from ennui and meaninglessness.

As a drifter, I'm speaking from experience, for I have spent most of my life roaming around. Yet, what I most desire now is to settle amid some lovely trees, away from other houses and the tight grid of streets, beginning to foster a sense of place where I belong. I long to remain rather than move on. To build relationships by staying in a place because I have chosen it as home and there is no other. I am ready to grow like the great trees that I adore, offering well-rooted shade and a contribution of something essential, if at times intangible, to the web of life in which we are all entwined.

Repeatedly, in some fashion or other, this journal explores the importance of opening our senses and heart, paying attention, and appreciating the ordinary sacred that surrounds us. Tirelessly, I advocate a communion with life because *everything is relationship*. Yet more and more I feel that such awareness must become *rooted*. To know that we belong to a place, selected because it nourishes in a significantly soulful way and that we are cultivating a sense of natural community, both human and *other*, is at least partly the cure for our listlessness.

We each need our place in the world, where our deeper creativity arises from that relationship and emerges *through* us.

C.G. Jung often remarked that his work in the world would not have been possible without his patch of earth, the stone tower he built at Bollingen on Lake Zurich. It was only because he had that singular place to nourish his soul that the wellspring of his vision and understanding could rise up and flow.

I feel the same. Or rather, that the future work coming through me depends entirely upon having a sense of deep-rooted connection to my place in nature. And yet, for a dozen mysterious reasons, we simply couldn't have dropped anchor earlier on the circuitous voyage, and I continue to have the very profound sense of being guided by mysterious currents, ones that I cannot even begin to fathom or understand.

"Not all who wander are lost," wrote J.R.R. Tolkien, a consolation and encouragement that I long ago took to heart.

It is close now, nearer than it has ever been, that sanctuary in the trees . The home that is calling me and that I am looking equally to meet, anxious to know it in my bones and breath as a lover, friend, and steward. The exact location, time schedule, and how it will arrive remains obscure; I am simply trying to be patient and focus on the tasks at hand.

All I know is that the potted lovelies on the front deck will be going with me, as surely as our two English Whippets. And it will be a place where my beloved and I can sit in rocking chairs on the front porch holding hands, watching the painted glow of sunset fade to periwinkle cast with diamond stars.

In the meantime, still here in a down-at-heel rented cottage near the sea, as I bless these dear, healing plants on the deck, perhaps I will purchase them some prettier pots to travel in.

❧ ❧ ❧

The Coyotes of Taos: Rewilding My Heart

(October, 2015)

I wake in the night to the voices of coyotes *yip yipping* outside.

The small casita where I am staying in Taos, New Mexico, is silent and dark, just a trickle of clouded moonlight seeping through curtained windows. The motorized whirl of the heater and hum of the refrigerator are both hushed, and for a few minutes the silvery darkness that enfolds me is rich and deep. Curled up in bed, hearing the canids, I am thrilled as a child on Christmas morning.

Welcome home.

From the sound of their voices, the shaggy wild ones are near, probably across the road in the open field near the little river, laughing and singing at the veiled, half-torn moon. For a moment I am tempted to throw back the covers and rise, to open the door and step outside to hear them better, but the gravity of the warm bed holds me fast and I simply lie there listening. Smiling. Feeling my heart unfurl its wide, feathered wings.

Driven out of my coastal California cottage by a familiar autumnal wanderlust, a lingering blue sadness, and the gentle prodding of a supportive mate who often recognizes my signs and symptoms better than I do, I have traveled to New Mexico. Heeding the strange tug and deep yearning to be among the golden cottonwoods, the fragrant piñon and sage at the foot of Taos Mountain, I've returned to this special place where I have resided twice previously in my life. It is a *soulscape* that brings me deeply alive, a world of pastel-hued earth and wide turquoise sky that remains forever lodged in my bones like an ancient chant. When I have been away too long, like some migratory impulse in my wild soul or a powerful spirit that beckons, I need to return to walk, sleep and dream at the foot of The Mountain.

There is nothing more sacred than a mountain.

I read those words somewhere years ago and they have lingered with me ever since. Here, the sentinel of Taos Mountain, protected and largely inaccessible on native pueblo land—its summit newly crowned with snow from the days of rain since my arrival, and now shrouded enigmatically in shifting clouds—looms over the town. Its presence is inescapable; a quietly grounding force that draws eyes, hearts, and

souls toward its mystery.
Sacred mountain. Warm casita. Wild, furry feet singing outside in the dark. Utterly brilliant, this.

I am blessed to be staying at the home of my dear friend who owns Casa Gallina, an artisan inn. The cluster of charmingly rustic, beautifully furnished adobe casitas is set amid gardens and an orchard on the rural west side of town. It is a handcrafted, alluring sanctuary featuring the work of local artists, where guests are greeted with a basket of freshly gathered eggs from the free-roaming hens (*gallina* is Spanish for "hen"), and Richard's inimitable style of being a host with heart. Everything at Casa Gallina urges visitors to slow down, to appreciate life and the beauty of Taos. My friend has a true dedication to eco-friendly and organic products, with a diligent eye to the sustainable and local, and these values mirror my own. It feels like no detail is overlooked here, and there is little that could warm my heart more than being in the welcoming home of a fellow Soul Artist.

Except maybe listening to the coyotes yipping at a cracked pearl of moon.

It is a sound that I always associate with dear old, dusty and muddy Taos. Both times that I dwelt here—first in the 90's in a shaman's adobe tower on the sage-strewn mesa, and years later in a jewel box casita on the Rio Grande del Rancho—the canids were a frequent and welcome presence in my life. I cannot count the nights I lay in my bed and listened to them laughing and serenading the darkness.

The Trickster in native legends, Coyote reminds me to not take it all so damn seriously. Always a welcome reminder for one who sometimes carries the weight of the world on his shoulders.

The feral ones near, hearing them again, feeds my own wild soul. Like birdsong, the susurrus of wind in the pines, or the high and low notes of a musical mountain stream, they are part of the song of the world—the one we can easily hear if we're paying attention. Almost none of us can catch the *other* song anymore, the deep music—the silent, wordless rejoicing of the animate earth *singing*, particularly at night and at dawn. The noise of the modern world is too great and we have shuttered our hearts, while simultaneously senses are dulled by the ongoing manmade commotion. Always I am grateful for the more easily heard wild voices, calling me home to myself.

Many times I have written of our innate connection to place, how we are never apart from our environment but rather *a part of.* Nothing is separate. For better or worse, we shape and are shaped by our surroundings, which reflect and also draw something forth within us. On the deepest level, when we are in harmony with a locale—literally, its energetic oscillation and frequency—our souls resonate with a compatible frequency. We feel harmonious and in alignment. We are open and at ease on a deep, cellular level.

At the core of our DNA, or at the whirling level of subatomic structure, *everything* is light and sound. (That sounds New Age but it's actually Nobel Prize–winning science.)

Taos (and northern New Mexico, in general) is one of the places where I most strongly resonate and feel in tune. It is somatic: a grounded connection in bones and breath, a quiet hum of power. I feel authentically myself, an openness and expansion mirrored by the landscape—*soulscape*—itself. Here, I am as much a part of the natural surroundings as the old adobe houses, the pale green chamisa and fragrant sagebrush, ebony ravens with guttural voices, copper rattlesnakes, lightning-ripped thunderstorms, the shimmering aspen trees, and wild sunflowers. Or those laughing coyotes with darkly glinting eyes.

Though my painted gypsy wagon has rolled far from this high desert plateau, it is always a blessing to return. I need to breathe and walk in a land that feels more wild than domesticated, where the song of the world can be heard, and everything sings me home to myself. A place where the power of earth and sky far outweighs the noisy impact of man and his notions of time. Body and soul are expansive here, an openness I find essential—like the pause between inhale and exhale, or the deep silence between heartbeats and stars.

I have written quite a bit on the Wild Soul (the better part of a book, actually) but lately I've been musing on *rewilding the heart*—particularly for men, who tend to place their seat of consciousness in the head rather than *bodysoul* or heart (much to the world's detriment). Too, I've been pondering the ways that we can facilitate that shift and essential awakening, particularly through cooperating with nature and learning a heart-centered attention. For when we are inspired, in tune, and receptive, the heart opens—inviting us to dance with life rather than conquer it.

In rewilding the heart, like any creature of nature, we become more authentic, passionate, embodied and free. At the same time, we draw closer to a new mythology and ancient wisdom that connects us to the larger story.

Rewilding the heart. That's what Taos does for me. It is not a cure all, this place, but as with a beautiful meal I am feeling well fed. Lying in bed and bathed in silvery moonlight, listening to coyotes join their yipping voices to the song of the world, a smile lingers on my face. I'm deeply content and grateful to be here, immersed in this *soulscape* that nourishes down to the warm, bright center of my being—from which I have been estranged.

Come and dance with the Trickster, why don't you.

Friend, I wonder, where is the place that draws and nourishes you? And how long since you have wandered there with heart and senses cast ajar? Maybe in the interest of connecting with your soul and rewilding your heart, it is time to return. To reunite with yourself.

Perhaps, if you're lucky, the wild ones will welcome you back home under a coyote moon.

ᘓ ᘓ ᘓ

Fresh Croissants and Plum Blossoms
(February, 2016)

I pocket the car key, don my wide-brimmed hat and rain jacket, and then slip out of the house with an early morning objective.

It is unusual that I drive anywhere before noon, even rarer to find me behind the wheel by 8:00 am, but this final day of a family member's visit, on a soggy grey morning, I am seized with the longing to serve fresh croissants and coffee. Wheat is a rarity in our house, but I am craving a proper, French-style patisserie offering—pastries that are buttery, flaky, and crisply shattering as you bite into them. To hell with healthy food. (For now.)

Mission accomplished, returning back over the hill with a box of freshly baked delights on the passenger seat beside me, the low grey clouds cling like a veil over the coastal landscape, draping the pines and cypress trees in silver mystery. It seems a fine day to sit indoors and write, that is, once I put my dear step-mom on the airport shuttle and then settle in to face the work I've set aside for the past six days of being a host. Time now to pick up my editor's pen and confront the stack of manuscript pages, crossing out and rewriting.

The household remains asleep except for two English Whippets who greet me at the door with keen interest and wagging tails—*you never take the car to go somewhere in the early morning, so hopefully you've returned with something tasty for us!* Noses upturned inquiringly, they are very intrigued by the low, square box in my hands, and follow me eagerly to the kitchen. Not having an automatic coffee maker, I set the kettle atop a blue flame to boil water for the brew, and then grind some organic, French roast beans—their darkly robust aroma instantly triggering a sense of morning goodness, despite that I am mostly a tea drinker.

When the boys realize there is nothing for them, dejectedly they return to bed, tails hung low, for it is raining and they have no desire to go outside. Pouring the hot water over the fragrant grinds, I wrap a tea towel around the glass cafetière to help keep it warm (years ago I owned a double-walled thermal one that did an admirable job of keeping liquids hot, but the thin glass was quite fragile and it broke). Opening the brown cardboard box affixed with the logo of Parker-Lusseau, an eager smile on my face, I select one of the golden croissants and place it on a small, hand thrown plate from a pottery kiln in West Sussex.

A fine treat, this. Seated at the table by the front window, my usual morning perch, I will savor an hour or so of quietude before the household finally rouses. An Italian hand-painted Deruta cup filled with fragrant coffee beside me, I tear the end from the croissant and gingerly place the torn segment into my mouth, savoring its buttery goodness, pleased how its outer shell crackles and crumbles. Frankly, unless you live in an urban zone with a quality patisserie, it's rare to find a well-made pastry in the States; they're always undercooked and flabby, rather than bronzed and shatteringly crisp on the outside.

I learned to make croissants and all manner of heavenly offerings during my studies at Le Cordon Bleu in Paris, and I truly enjoy the extended process of making "laminated" pastries; creating a yeasted dough that is then rolled out with layers of butter, folded, and rolled out again (and again), with extended periods of rest between each stage. Once cut and rolled, the crescents need to be "proofed" (given time to rise a bit) and brushed lightly with an egg wash, a glaze that when baked becomes the golden exterior that helps make them flaky. They are meant to be eaten *fresh*, not after having sat around for hours or a day.

Like puff pastry, or the two-day, artisan *pain au levain* I used to craft, the results are entirely worth the effort (and hours of waiting), I say. Alas that my little 1980's kitchen here at the cottage, with only a small rectangle of old, tiled counter space simply isn't adequate for the task of *viennoiserie*. And then there's the fact that I simply don't bake much anymore, having given up wheat except for rare occasions like this morning, or my yearly pilgrimage to France, the Holy Land of *boulangers*.

Nibbling the flaky croissant, sipping strong coffee in a colorful cup, I stare aimlessly through the front windows at the rainy morning, feeling simultaneously content with the treat of breakfast and slightly overwhelmed by the task facing me. Like any large project, the enormous effort, discipline and commitment of creating a worthwhile book feels daunting at times. The actual writing of my latest manuscript wasn't difficult—a memoir about living in England, it poured from my pen in a mere three weeks, filling two notebooks with jumbled black script— but the subsequent job of typing and editing, and then re-editing, feels anything but inspired. Word by word, sentence by sentence, it is solitary and mostly tedious *work*.

There is a part of me that just wishes it to be done, to move on to something more creative. And yet, as with life, to focus simply upon the distant destination is to miss the details of the actual journey. Good things take time. To fashion something of beauty requires patience, whether that be a croissant, sculpture, painting, a tapestry, a music album, a house, a book. Or simply a well-lived, authentic existence.

I have written previously about *soul projects:* an investment in something that is larger than ourselves, a creation or endeavor that shares a certain aspect of your soul in a meaningful way. Soul projects are a commitment to our true work in the world; delivering the unique gift that each of us has to offer. The goal isn't simply about finishing but rather investing in the process itself—like raising children, creating and tending a garden, building an organization or community, or committing to one's personal transformation and growth.

For a while now, I've had a self-imposed deadline looming in my head, a date by which I want to be able to show this new manuscript to an editor (whom an author friend has invited me to meet). Yet I realize that hurrying through the work will only yield a result that feels rushed. Better to trust in the mysterious process, the strangely glimmering thread that leads from one event to the next, a day at a time, sometimes only one step after another (I was just reminded of this in a curious, vivid dream).

Savoring the hushed cottage while the household still sleeps, musing on soul projects, and gazing into the rainy front garden, my eye is drawn to the two small, ornamental plum trees near the fence that have recently burst into bright bloom. Their naked, spindly branches are adorned in inch-wide ruffled pink pompoms of soft spun silk, each with a garnet center. On a grey, wet morning, it is a wordless riot of color and exuberance.

Appreciating the stunning display of nature's elegance and creativity, I am silently reminded, *each thing in its own time.* Mysterious currents and events guide us to bloom, and yet even a lovely blossom, fair as it may be, is not the end result, for the flower eventually becomes fruit, one that then goes on as seed to begin the cycle anew.

Yes, editing my manuscript feels tedious and large, and perhaps it won't be even remotely ready to show an editor until autumn, which seems ages away. So be it. In the moment, my only real task is to show up fully for the day, senses wide open and welcoming, appreciating whatever beauty and grace is present. I have a delicious, flaky croissant on a hand-glazed plate, a fine cup of strong coffee (a pleasant change of pace from my usual 'cuppa'), and a soft rain falls outside to nourish the earth. Soon there will be breakfast with my dear stepmom and my mate, a couple of English Whippets underfoot. Later, a bodywork client or two to help pay the bills. And a pile of pages that, like a sculptor with mallet and chisel, my pen will work steadily upon.

Breathing in, breathing out. Savoring the little, ordinary moments of the day—the way they feel in hand or linger within my heart, singing softly.

Show up at the page, my friend, whatever such work may be for you. Open your senses. Wriggle your bare toes down into damp soil. Laugh. Celebrate. Feed the birds. Chip away at the stone. And while you're at it, find some flaky bits of buttery goodness to nibble on while you appreciate the fleeting flowers—the ones that wait patiently for you and the amber honeybees to notice them.

Each thing in its own time, quietly growing and transforming, all while we spiral forward on this blue-green jewel of a planet.

Blessed be.

☙ ☙ ☙

The Outermost House: A Writer's Year on Cape Cod

(January, 2015)

I love books that are like a fine meal, read slowly and savored. Disappointingly, it is far too rare that I encounter one, whether fiction or non-fiction. I don't frequently venture into fiction realms these days (though I used to devour shelves of it), largely because I am so very particular about what I desire to read—or experience, rather, because that is what good writing is. A well-written work immerses readers in word and image, guiding us into a different room or realm, and, at its best, delivers a *felt* sensation that moves in some way.

I keep thinking I'd like to get back into reading fiction, but when I pick up novels at a bookstore, after reading the rear cover synopsis or thumbing through the pages, I end up simply laying the book back down and moving on. Often the writing fails to spark my interest, or the story seems overly contrived, following a predetermined method and predictable arc of plot, even in a supposedly character-driven novel.

Among writers there is an unspoken sentiment that to craft *real* or worthy fiction, it must be serious. There seems to be an ongoing, strong trend towards the tragic these days, a disaster required in the pages as part of the novel's formula—an assumption that people need something intense to hook and maintain their interest, or to actually feel. I don't mind serious or weighty, but the tragic holds little allure for me. The books that I most like to read, the quietly moving story in beautiful prose, or an artful tale that uplifts and inspires, these are rare gems.

Thus, most often I find myself reading non-fiction. Not because it necessarily moves or delivers me to another realm but I do find a wider band of books to enjoy, and generally I am less looking for a literary experience. (That said, as surely as with novels, an art exists to good non-fiction writing.)

Amid the non-fiction ranks, one of my favorite genres is that of the personal narrative: a chronicle as told through a person's direct experience. The best ones are written with an engaging voice and descriptive eye, and as with skilled fiction, summon us into the territory of *feeling*. I tend to enjoy personal stories about nature, living abroad in a foreign country, fixing up an old house at the end of a road, or the work and pleasures of a garden and cooking with the bounty it yields; narratives that reflect some aspect(s) of quiet, soulfully engaged living and observation. *Pilgrim At Tinker Creek* by Annie Dillard, which won the Pulitzer

Prize, is one I have returned to over and over, and always survives the repeated culling of my bookshelves as a wandering nomad.

So it was with great delight that I learned of *The Outermost House* from my friend, the poet Carolyn Brigit Flynn, when she and her wife (who is also a fine poet) came for dinner one evening at my little writer's studio. Hearing about the book and how dear it was to her, a woman who loves well spun words and weaves them masterfully herself, I knew instantly that I needed to obtain a copy.

❧

Written in 1928, the narrative details the solitary year spent by author Henry Beston in a tiny cottage on the eastern shore of Cape Cod. He called it the *Fo'castle* but it was dubbed the Outermost House because it was simply that: built upon a high dune on the great beach of the outermost Cape, only other dunes and marshland around it, and nothing beyond except the wide grey Atlantic.

The thirty-something year old Beston went originally in September to spend two weeks at the two-room cottage, its total dimensions just twenty by sixteen feet, with a fireplace for heat.

> *"The fortnight ending, I lingered on, and as the year lengthened into autumn, the beauty and mystery of this earth and outer sea so possessed and held me that I could not go."*

Though it has never achieved the fame of Thoreau's works, *The Outermost House* is a quiet classic of American nature writing. Pioneer environmentalist Rachel Carson, author of *Silent Spring*, claimed Beston's work was the only book that influenced her writing. Reading the pages of elegantly written words, it is not hard to understand why. Here is a record of quiet observation, a keen-eyed discovery of the elemental world that enfolded the author—a study of changing tides, wind and clouds, migrating birds, and shifting moods of light and weather in the solar ritual of a year.

In 1964, Beston's small, rustic cottage was proclaimed a National Literary Landmark. During a great winter storm in 1978, the Outermost House was swept away and perished, though many of its humble relics (such as Henry's wooden writing chair) were salvaged.

Beston conveys a compelling sense of the natural drama that enfolded him, a restless sea and mutable land, a wild and unsullied realm utterly independent and oblivious of mankind. There is a young man's sense of discovery within the pages, looking intently at the world and reveling in the delight he feels for it. The focus is decidedly out there rather than inward or introspective, yet he clearly senses the importance of wild nature for our human souls:

> *"The world today is sick to its thin blood for lack of elemental things, for fire before the hands, for water welling up from the earth, for air, for the dear earth itself underfoot... The longer I stayed, the more eager was I to know this coast and to share its mysterious and elemental life."*

Nearly a century old, the language is exquisite and the young author's powers of description are formidable. Eloquently and evocatively, he captures his undomesticated world with a kinesthetic touch and a full engagement of the senses. I am utterly seduced and transported away.

☙

In the quiet of an early morning, seated in the alcove of windows of my rented writing studio, bathed in pale winter light and listening to the dull chant of the ocean though the old glass panes, I too am at the edge of the world, apprenticing to tides and shifting light. I have read it as I do all wonderful books—slowly, not more than a chapter a day, sipping the experience like a well crafted wine.

Yet beyond the enviable skill of his writing, what has most moved me about Beston's narrative is how strikingly different the world is nowadays. In our brightly lit, fast-paced, and noisy existence, few can imagine a life like Henry's solitary year on the Cape; no electricity, warmth only from a fire, and no modern diversions like television, radio or Internet, only the deep wordlessness of nature suffusing the days. Indeed, to the restless and distracted, his descriptions of spending from sunrise to sunset simply observing the world around him—birds, surf, clouds, insects, weather—and long strolls of walking the ever-changing beach, constitute a very foreign realm.

> *"From the moment that I rose in the morning and threw open my door looking toward the sea to the moment when the spurt of a match sounded in the evening quiet of my little house, there was always something to do, something to observe, something to record, something to study, something to put aside in a corner of the mind."*

An unhurried pace and the ability to give our attention fully to something as an artist would—to really see it—this too has become unfamiliar territory. Most of us, after even a few hours in nature, as we call it, are ready for our familiar diversions once more. Disengaged from near-constant, chosen distractions or social exchanges, we are quickly bored and restless. Anxious, even. To spend an entire day alone on the land, simply walking and observing, perhaps writing in a journal, is far beyond the modern, shortened grasp and inclinations. And to do such a thing for weeks upon end, for months stitched into the long "ritual" of a year..? Nearly everyone I know would feel crazy after two days of such an existence (though by the gods, it would be good for them).

Once a week, at a predetermined time, Henry would traverse up to the distant road and meet a friend for a ride into town, where he would buy supplies and engage in a bit of socialization. Then he returned carrying his goods (coffee, flour, eggs, sugar) in a rucksack as he hiked through the whispering, shifting dunes to his modest retreat at the threshold of earth, sea, and sky.

Admittedly, I feel a certain resonance and kinship with Beston's deep comfort in solitude. To be at ease with our own silent company and that of the wild world— we are never really alone, after all—is a rare, invaluable thing. Many of us are running from our demons (or simply trying to keep them medicated); alone and isolated, however, they draw quickly near.

I value my solitude. Honestly, I become a bit unhinged when I don't have a good amount of it. Though the worlds are strikingly different in environment, reading *The Outermost House,* I am reminded of my first period of living in Taos, New Mexico, when in my early twenties I resided alone for six months on the wild sagebrush-covered mesa in an adobe tower. It was five miles down a deeply rutted dirt road, with no phone, television, or radio (though I had electricity and water from a deep well). My retreat was a profound and transforming time, one that altered the course of my life in a subtle but dramatic way. (On a long journey, if you shift your course just a few degrees early on, you'll find yourself at a very different destination.) It was in the extended period of deep solitude that my senses truly started to unfurl, when as a city-raised person I began to engage the natural, living world in a different way than ever before—with a heart and soul wide open to wonder. And it was then I learned that I had a secret name, one that only the wind, trees and stars knew... they being the ones who gave it to me.

When you navigate with your soul, when you live with an unshuttered heart, things affect you deeply. That, of course, is why most people avoid it whenever possible. Yet therein lies the beauty of being fully human, of becoming a full-spectrum being, one who embraces and values both the uplifting joys and heavy sorrows in life.

I am indebted for the gift of Henry Beston's lovely book. (Thank you again, Carolyn.) It has gently inspired me with both its remarkable language and astute observations of the 'more-than-human' world, leading me on a journey to a much quieter time and place where I feel curiously at home in the richly woven solitude. Too, it stirs the misty blue longing I carry to be even more connected to the conscious symphony that enfolds us, the living "web pulse of life," and offer it my ongoing, wordless attention. Awe. Praise and gratitude.

Soul Artists endeavor to live with their senses wide open. As I have written before, we are engaged in a polysensory love affair with the world. Too, we realize that what is *out there* is also *in here*, for we are never really separate: everything is relationship. Such individuals also understand that in solitude we draw nearest to ourselves, and if we allow the restless waters to settle and become still, we see our true reflection gazing up from the depths. Stepping away from the endless rattle and hum, more clearly we hear the small voice that guides us to the deeper truths we seek––which are everywhere, simply waiting to reveal themselves to us.

Gentle reader, here's hoping that you encounter something this week that inspires or moves you. A book. A poem. A moment of unexpected beauty or tenderness that pierces to the core. Even a deep blue sadness. Whatever it is, may it steer you gently towards opening the shutters of your heart, welcoming the world in a bold and an undefended way. Pause to savor it, senses cast wide. Breathe.

Beston's book is not one of action, dialogue, or even story; it is a testament to observation. We are only passing through, each of us. A book like *The Outermost House* compels one to ask:

To what will we give the gift of our attention?

❧ ❧ ❧

Becoming Visible: The Risk to Grow

(May, 2016)

The long green leaf of the orchid in the kitchen window has unfurled like a dark, shiny tongue, a precursor, I hope, to a new spike of dazzling purple blossoms.

I stood at the sink admiring it, my hands in warm soapy water as I washed the dishes after supper, while appreciating too the newly installed faucet, that only this morning replaced its leaking, thirty-year old predecessor. A quiet moment of tranquility, often a ritual of gentle mindfulness for me [read, "Washing the Dishes, Tending the Earth"], except that I was churning with angst.

Last week, I took a bold step and sent the early draft of my unpublished manuscript, "Fields, Foxes and Tea," to two friends for perusal. Having an early reader(s) is new territory for me and feels vulnerable, like walking on stony ground with bare, tender feet. Though they have only just received the pages, two days ago I began my next round of edits on the initial chapters, gutting entire paragraphs and sections, and I've been gripped by remorse that it was too soon to share the work. The draft is too workmanlike, and I should never have let it out of my clutches, even to someone trusted.

Oh, the folly of it all. Yet it was only a few weeks ago that I wrote a post inspired by a quote from Welsh-born poet David Whyte, a reflection on inhabiting our vulnerability, and choosing the ways we become more visible. In letting the early draft be read by others, I was certainly "walking my talk."

My inner critic laments that they will see at last that I am not a real writer but merely an imposter, and I will be exposed for my utter lack of skill: passive voice; repetitive sentence structure; poor punctuation skills; a mishmash of British and American spellings; repeated use of pet words; unable to decide what is superfluous and what has real grit; inconsistent voice; rambling descriptions that "tell" but don't "show" while leading nowhere in advancing the story; *ad nauseum.*

Angst ... a cold hand squeezing my guts and slowly forcing the breath out of me.

As if it weren't uncomfortable enough to have friends seeing my naked draft for all its flaws, an internationally famous author on the other side of the world is simultaneously doing the same. What a brazen, impatient fool am I.

The yellow sponge in my hand caressed the large dinner plate's painted design of Turkish flowers, and part of me wanted to simply submerge my head in the sudsy water to drown the anguished chatter. At the very least, I wished that I could grab back the copies of the manuscript and remain in safe territory where I could quietly *polish, polish, polish*—until the work gleams like untarnished silver, and only *then* offering it forward with a sense of modest worth and pride.

It is risky enough to pen a memoir, a venture that so easily tips into narcissism—the "ME-moir"—a trap I have tried to avoid. Ultimately, any book that I write needs to be about something larger than simply me (or us), it must sing to the larger story and the reasons we are alive. *All of us.*

"It will tell something remarkable. It will be beautifully executed. It will be nested in truth." Words of Barbara Kingsolver, they are written on an old piece of paper pinned next to my desk, a gentle reminder for what I hope to accomplish. A wide-open roadmap of sorts.

Gently scrubbing a turquoise-glazed, hand thrown mug while reflecting what my two friends and the famous author were currently reading, I couldn't feel further from said writing goal. And yet, awash in my clamorous anguish and vulnerability, I simultaneously felt beautifully human. Flawed and perfect in the same shining moment, fully inhabiting my exposed authenticity.

Words do not always flow inspired and sparkling from my pen; more often they are clunky, slow and lifeless. Better, I think, to simply get them down on paper and refine them later than to sit fishing and anguishing for a single beautiful line. Still, how impetuous of me to share this early work. Dumb, really.

I wanted to send an urgent message to my friends: "Change of plan. Please burn and destroy *BEFORE* reading, not after."

I have set nearly everything in my life aside to embrace this work with words, but perhaps I have too much invested in being a *writer,* or an artist, rather than simply *being.* Just this morning, after waking from a powerfully auspicious dream, an email arrived from my author friend in Italy, gently encouraging the same idea—less attachment and angst, more being—and to *trust.*

So, onward I go with pages and pen in hand, a cup of green tea beside me, endeavoring to create something of beauty and honest vulnerability that touches the soul. Reminding myself that even great cathedrals are built simply from stones, chiseled and laid one at a time by rough hands, a work that took years (lifetimes, even) to complete.

Friend, as I wrote a few weeks ago in the post, "Inhabiting our Vulnerability":

> *"Each day a hundred opportunities exist to play it safe, to hold back, to turn away from that quiet inner voice that whispers the bare truth. Step into the circle of authenticity instead, the ring of Soul Artists."*

There is no real safety in the world, it is mostly an illusion. And we can never freely move, dance, make love, or live fully when wearing our armor. Equally true for writing.

The dear orchid on the windowsill doesn't lament or fret that its newly unfolded leaf isn't good enough, long or shiny enough, it simply keeps on growing—even now summoning its energy to put forth a new display of stunning flowers. How simple, really. It is only we humans who make things complicated, always forgetting there is but one true imperative:

Grow.

❧ ❧ ❧

Changing Seasons: Feeling the Touch of the World
(September, 2016)

I wonder sometimes if I am simply dreaming this life, or whether I am being *dreamed,* instead.

In the past weeks, England has been heavily in my mind. At unexpected moments throughout the day—washing and cutting vegetables, walking the dogs, taking a shower—I suddenly *see* myself there, mostly back in places familiar to me. A feeling and affect suddenly washes over, sometimes a scent as well. The oddest bit is that sometimes I see myself in places there that I *don't yet* know, though it is clear from the landscape that these too are Britain; the look, feel, and sense of them is unmistakable for one who has lived in the United Kingdom. It's difficult to explain, really. I've even wondered whether I am seeing the future, or if some parallel reality is somehow converging with the one I normally inhabit during my waking hours.

For a long time, I've been something of a reluctant mystic. I've been a "sensitive" since childhood, though in recent years some of these modes of heightened awareness seem to be increasing. They are gifts that have supported my healing work with others, and such experiences as these recent episodes are not altogether unusual for me. Yet mostly such "impressions" arise when I am in a quiet, meditative, and receptive state, as with working with clients or immersed in wild nature, and I find it curious that Britain is suddenly so prevalent in my everyday consciousness—as if it's somehow being broadcast into me.

In the past, I've wrestled with how much I want to reveal of these gifts. I have resisted talking or writing about them, because they tend to be misunderstood by others and easily attract projection. Personally, I believe that we ALL have the ability to perceive in such a heightened manner; it's simply that, for most people, the sensory gating channels are habitually narrowed to a very small range, and the necessary circuitry isn't activated. Despite an innate aptitude, over the last twenty years I have *learned* to be this way—or perhaps better to say I've more fully opened these channels and begun to *trust* what comes through (which is actually the most difficult). Coming from somewhere beyond, this non-ordinary way of knowing arises mostly from the heart; it's entirely non-rational and deeply somatic, and thus at odds with the linear, deductive, mental mode so prized in our society.

Clairvoyance. Clairsentience. Clairaudience. People often imagine that such abilities would be a great boon. I assure you that this type of knowing also comes *heavily* loaded with challenges, not the least of which is that when you live with channels wide open, the modern world often feels utterly overwhelming. Unlivable, even. Hence my deep need for the solace and healing I find in wild places, where the soft touch of a million invisible strands support and cradle as they wordlessly remind me what is true.

Yet in censoring my writing about experiences that others may not understand or find challenging to accept and believe, I withhold part of my essence from the larger story. *None of us serve the world by choosing to remain small or safe*—especially because safety is mostly an illusion.

I wrote a few weeks ago in "The Shaman of Stars," *dare to tell the truth, even if others won't understand.* So be it. Here on the central California coast, I've been slipping in and out of an ongoing feeling and image stream of being in Europe, nearly as if I am in two places at once.

Tucked into the fog pocket of this peninsula, the past four months have passed with perhaps ten days of sunshine in total. *Gloomy* would be an understatement. It was a few days ago that I felt the first, early touch of autumn approaching: a slight shift in the air and its taste/scent, accompanied by a barely perceptible weakening of the light. Driving over the hill to Whole Foods Market in Monterey, I noted the first trees gilded with gold, and I thought, oh my, autumn is on the doorstep and we never even had *summer.*

Yet not long afterwards, as I stood outside on the deck, gazing up at the Grandmother Monterey cypress, watching her hundreds of lacy green hands wave delicately in the coastal breeze, feeling the faint brush of autumn upon my skin, my despair over the endless summer gloom suddenly vanished. It was as if a small golden key turned in its lock with a soft, audible *click* and a gate swung open, inviting me across the threshold into a hidden garden that I know and love.

Here in the Northern Hemisphere, as the harvest moon wanes from its partial eclipse, the autumnal equinox (Mabon in neopagan traditions) looms just days away, and we will officially drift into Fall, as Americans call it. My favourite season.

An unabashed sensualist, I celebrate each cycle of the year for what it brings, yet the painted melancholy of autumn never fails to strum harmonic chords in my soul. Appetite and cooking both change, spiraling back towards warming stews and something simmering fragrantly at the rear of the stove—*au coin du feu*, the French would say, a certain nostalgic expression—filling the house with a sense of gustatory delight. As if on cue, I find myself ready to bake fresh apple tarts with shatteringly crisp, buttery pastry, and craving my seven-day duck *confit*, a labour of love (and good taste) that always catapults me back to my school year in France.

The other afternoon, in a familiar ritual, I found myself reaching for *The Kitchen Diaries II* on the bookshelf, one of several works by Nigel Slater, arguably Britain's best food writer, and reading through September's recipes, with a brewed "cuppa" from the Tea Palace (my preferred tea shop in London) beside me. Later, as I stood by the window and gazed out at a low grey sky, I felt the soft tug at my heart—the yearning for a long walk through misty woods and fields as I used to in West Sussex, a charcoal cashmere scarf wrapped around my neck, threading along footpaths strewn with burnished leaves, occasionally kicking the green, spiky hulls of horse chestnuts *(conkers,* the Brits call them) with my boots. And I recalled the goodness of returning to our cottage after such a countryside ramble, there to curl up with a warm mug of spiced apple cider, its steam heady with notes of cinnamon and clove.

I cannot adequately explain this strange presence of England I've been feeling, seeing, and sensing; neither *how* it arrives nor *why*. It is decidedly different than daydreaming, recalling, or merely imagining. The curious flashes and images continue unabated; indeed, they seem to be intensifying as autumn approaches, and as I roll along with a sense of nostalgia, I can only wonder what it all means.

Possibly, it has simply to do with the fact that this is the first year since coming back to America in 2011 that we have not returned to Europe for a visit, and I am simply missing the Old World. Yet I think perhaps something deeper and more mysterious is afoot, related to the expansive, healing shift I've been going through these past months. Something mystic. Shamanic, even.

Visions aside, what I do know is that most evenings this week have found me wanting something very French to eat—such as a perfectly roasted, organic chicken swaddled in a rich sauce of white wine, cream, and shallots. Mushrooms, perhaps. Admittedly, as much as I dearly miss the UK, or appreciate Nigel Slater's food writing, my culinary preferences dwell elsewhere. You can take the cook out of France, but not the other way around. In years past, this seasonal juncture would mark the time that I shift from those summer white and rosé wines to Pinot Noir (Oregon or Old World, thank you) but, as part of my healing path, I haven't had a glass since March six months ago. Even more strangely, I don't miss it. (Well, perhaps Champagne... just a bit.)

Each season brings treasures and trials, rolling away into mists of memory just before we tire of it. In an endless cycle of birth, maturing, and passing away, the wheel rolls on and something new arrives. Autumn approaches (while spring is waking up for those Down Under), bringing a timely shift and the endless offering of goodness that we too easily take for granted. Already I am dreaming of crisp, rosy-skinned apples, squat pumpkins and hearty winter squash, glistening chestnuts, milky sweet walnuts, and the earthy allure of wild mushrooms.

Friend, a liminal time descends upon us, a bountiful harvest amid the painted, graceful dying to what came before. A perfume of woodsmoke lingers in the cool air. It is naturally a season for memories and nostalgia, of slow turning inwards. The time comes to let things go, mirrored so eloquently for us by the noble trees and our gardens.

As summer bows out and autumn sweeps onstage, open the doors of perception. Cast them wide as you unlock the heart, and welcome whatever comes through. Surrender to shifting nuances of light, scent and feeling. Memory, perhaps, or a future sense. And through those unbridled senses, may you feel the soft but indelible touch of the world, reminding you to pause and appreciate its endless wonders, great and small. For despite all the chaos, madness, and troubles that clamour too loudly in harsh, angry tones, we are simultaneously immersed in a natural world and larger story that is achingly beautiful. Mysterious and magical, too.

I wonder, are we dreaming or awake? Perhaps if the heart is unshuttered and ajar, they are nearly the same.

ॐ ॐ ॐ

Winter Solstice: A Holiday Ritual
(December, 2014)

The stockings are hung by the old stone chimney with care.

Below them upon the hand-carved hearth, a pair of tall white candles glow warmly, and a large poinsettia in front of the fireplace (soon to be moved for this evening's fire) adds a bit of holiday cheer to my little poet's cottage. Even if I had the space in this cozy writer's retreat (and I most certainly don't), you wouldn't find a proper tree here—I swore off cut evergreen trees years ago. Instead, a miniature potted cypress, only a foot high and festooned with three special childhood ornaments, sits quaintly on the round table that doubles both as a dining area and my writing desk in an alcove of windows.

Here on the blustery Central California coast, welcoming some winter storms that bring desperately needed rain, I'm feeling rather festive. I am decidedly under the influence of more cheer than I've managed to summon in the last few rounds of year-end holidays in Hawaii, where it never feels much like the classic Christmas—you know, the holly, ivy, and evergreen sort. No, there it seems just like any other day in the subtropics. Apart from lights wrapped around the coconut palm trees, 25 December could be Easter or Fourth of July. And while I am somewhat reluctantly heading back to the islands for Christmas once more, I hope to carry with me a bit of the holiday spirit I've been feeling lately.

In the minuscule kitchen (akin to a galley on a sailboat), a pot of Moroccan-inspired chicken stew simmers quietly at the rear of the cooker, with enticing, faintly exotic notes of cumin and cinnamon wafting through the cottage. My partner is here, enjoying a much needed break and a bit of mainland holiday cheer. In the social spirit of the season, we've enjoyed a couple of nice dinners with friends, both new and old, the gatherings all pleasantly subdued and tasteful in the very best way.

I bowed out of gift-buying madness even longer ago than I gave up having a proper holiday tree. I wanted to simplify Christmas, and I do not know a single person who needs more 'stuff'. The few presents that I now give to others tend to be experiences that can be shared: a pair of concert tickets; dinner at a nice restaurant; a gift certificate for a massage; something homemade and freshly baked; perhaps something for the cook, like a bottle of artisan olive oil. Or an artful wine.

Sadly, Americans have largely tossed aside the notion of *less is more* (we are not alone in this but arguably the worst). The collective thinking seems to be that if we make Christmas even bigger and better, it will somehow recapture its magic and meaning. Certainly that's what the retailers and advertisers want us to believe, but I beg to differ. In my opinion, keeping the holidays *simpler* enables them to mean more; decidedly it makes them far more enjoyable.

Here and there I detect a growing unhappiness with the ever-increasing commercialization of Christmas, a pervasive grumbling at holiday merchandise and decorations set out in October, but it's not simply the advertisers' or merchants fault—we are the ones rushing out to buy. The so-called Black Friday after Thanksgiving is a national embarrassment, I think—from stores opening at midnight, to the hordes of people lined up to stampede for bargains. The real magic of Christmas is not something that can be bought, folks. It is up to us as individuals to make decisions that simplify the holidays, reorganize our priorities, and keep the focus on something more meaningful than an escalation of mad spending, soulless parties, and more *stuff.* (Stands down from soapbox.)

I have wonderful Christmas memories from childhood. My mother was the very spirit of the season: ever generous, tasteful and classy, and very fond of wrapping presents and giving thoughtful, well-chosen gifts. When she died more than two decades ago, I stepped away from traditional Christmas completely. For several years, I simply couldn't face it and I took an extended break, neither giving nor receiving presents. When I finally decided to rediscover and reinvent the holidays, I chose to celebrate winter solstice rather than Christmas proper. I couldn't subscribe to any notion of celebrating Jesus's birthday, but I could rejoice in the gradually lengthening days and return of the sun and warmth. A lovely present or two exchanged with my beloved felt nice, so I welcomed that, too.

Stepping out of the traditional, often crazy "holidaze" and creating my own traditions has been tremendously freeing and empowering. I genuinely enjoy the holiday season now but mostly because it is entirely on my terms. And as I said, I keep things *simple.*

Not that I needed any validation in creating my own rituals, but living abroad in different countries over the years, I realized that many traditions exist around Christmas, even down to the day gifts are given. Celebrating *Joyeaux Noël,* the French exchange presents clear through to Epiphany, 6 January (though Epiphany varies in different countries). In Spain and much of Europe, it is Christmas Eve that's the big night, followed later by Three Kings (Epiphany) as the grand culmination of two weeks of celebration. During our years in England, I enjoyed Boxing Day, usually December 26—unless the day after Christmas falls on a weekend, at which point Boxing Day is Monday, the first workday following. It's a bank holiday and nearly everything is shut, with limited train service, which essentially makes Christmas into a two-day event. Rather than a brief twenty-four hours capping a month-long buying frenzy, Christmas gets extended into something that feels like a proper holiday. Boxing Day gets its own food and gatherings, too, if decidedly less grand and more relaxed than the day previous.

In the Northern Hemisphere, the December solstice marks the longest night of the year, when darkness reaches its full glory. For years, I celebrated the winter solstice not only as a neo-pagan alternative to traditional Christmas but also to celebrate the light returning in a bleak winter. Like our ancestors of old, the advent of days growing lengthier and the dark slowly retreating seemed as worthy a thing to raise a toast to as anything else.

It was probably a decade ago that I started hosting an annual winter solstice feast at our house; an intimate sit-down dinner for friends and family, an all-out affair employing the old silver and good china. Wherever we roamed on the globe, at the festively decorated dinner table, to my assembled guests I would usually make a little speech about the pagan origins of the winter solstice, the Roman celebrations of Saturnalia and Sol Invictus, and how Pope Julian 1 moved the "Christ mass" to coincide with the largest pagan holiday of the year, arguably to gain more followers for Christianity.

More recently, reflecting my ongoing work with soul, around the time that we moved to England, I made a curious switch in the focus of my December solstice fête—celebrating the darkness itself. As the realm of soul and mystery, of transforming Underworld journeys, and the cocoon for symbolic death and rebirth, I decided to welcome and celebrate the darkness rather than pushing it away as something undesirable (or rejoice in its demise).

In *The Bones & Breath,* at the outset of the chapter "Myth, Shadow and Light," I share:

> *"Most celebrations of the Winter Solstice focus upon the light returning but on this snowy night I'm choosing to celebrate the darkness, itself. Rather than something to be pushed away, I'm keen to welcome and embrace it. As an integral part of the Cosmos and psyche, the richness of the dark is both essential and misunderstood.*

Darkness is more than merely the absence of light; the dark holds its own unique energy, a powerful and palpable force in its own right. It guards something vital and mysterious. It is the hushed breath of lovers and the elemental force to tear them apart. Like either the Sacred Masculine or Divine Feminine, the dark embodies one half of creation. Truly, light loses its significance without the opposite to offer contrast and balance...

... Even as we fear or associate it with death, darkness is essential for creation, new life, and rebirth. A seed only sprouts when placed under a protective and nurturing layer of soil with the light blocked away. When the masculine spark seeds the feminine womb of creation—in the Unified Field, the energetic spheres of psyche and deep imagination, or in physical reproduction—it is in darkness that life and energy generates. Gestation is an essential time of growth; a time of sacred waiting before birth where profound change and transformation is occurring but cannot yet be seen. In such darkness, energies evolve into molecules and matter; cells divide and create new forms; seeds germinate and reach upwards towards their potential; bees build their sacred geometry of comb and turn the nectar and pollen of flowers into honey; and events draw mysteriously together to form pathways, destinies, and solar systems."

The fecundity of darkness is elemental. And worthy of its own celebration, I say.

As an aside note, whilst living in England, no, I never joined the massive solstice gatherings at Stonehenge—upwards of twenty thousand pagans and partygoers in attendance. Mobbed and mad is *never* my scene, and when you toss in being outdoors for a long night in freezing cold weather, well... no thank you. Far better to remain at home in our cozy countryside cottage, and invite some friends over for a festive dinner and tall crystal flutes of good bubbly.

Another aside note, I will confess to liking the clever sign: *Axial tilt is the reason for the season.* I fancy it for a t-shirt, personally.

Given our ongoing existence as nomads, and my spending as much time away from the islands as possible (mainland people just don't understand), I'm not hosting a solstice dinner this year. I will miss it, but I trust that there will be future times to gather with friends at an elegant table and share the bounty and blessings of a season. Feasting and generosity is certainly part of the art of life, one that I embrace and celebrate, and perhaps my feast will happen in summertime, instead.

Christmas looms imminent—full of cheer, the chaos of rampant consumerism, and little twinkling lights. The darkness reaches its depths and begins a slow retreat, even as we spiral into the stark fullness of winter. Surely we can all find something to celebrate. A candle shines brightest in the shadows, and yet the dark offers its own gifts, ones too often missed by those who chase only the light.

Soul Artists know that we always have an abundance to be grateful for, even amidst our seeming troubles. Simple treasures abound through the day in any season, given freely to those who are paying attention through open senses. While any time of year is the right time to unlatch our hearts, the holidays seem to be a special period to do so, a time when we are met more freely by others doing the same.

Gentle reader, here's hoping that you find unique and special ways to savor these winter holidays in a manner that truly nourishes your soul. Unapologetically start a new tradition. Boldly bow out of whatever doesn't feed your spirit. With whomever and however we choose to celebrate, may we all remember that it's actually a season of *gratitude* and *sharing*. My wish is that we can all practice kindness and share the very best of what we have.

Whether in darkness or light, may you receive and welcome the mysterious grace and priceless gifts of this journey as an embodied soul.

A New Year: Spiraling into Possibility

(January, 2016)

I'm not generally one for New Year's parties or ringing in another calendar year in a boisterous, social way. No, I would prefer to be peacefully at home (or pleasantly on holiday) and tucked into bed by the time midnight rolls around.

With my partner gone to a soirée that I predictably bowed out of, I sat quietly in our little cottage, a favorite pen and little black journal in hand, reflecting upon the year. Pleasantly soft music played in the background, candles flickered on the hearth and in the windows, a flute of nice bubbly sparkled beside me, and I considered both the good and not-so-good of the past twelve months.

Personally, I'm not sorry to close the door on 2015. This latest trip round the sun was a difficult one on many levels, and I'm looking forward to a more nurturing year ahead as we spiral on. That's what I'm hoping for, anyway. Certainly there were gifts and grace that manifested in this first year of having a book in the world, of stepping into a new identity as *author,* but frankly much of the passage felt like a struggle.

There is a normal tendency at the close and opening of a year, I think, to look back and forward, along with a desire to bid *adieu* to the past cycle and begin anew. As if we can just wipe the slate clean. After all, don't we simply open a new calendar and/or change the last digit(s) of the year when we write it out? Perhaps.

It looks so neat and orderly, those monthly arrangements of boxes representing days; seven in a row, four stacked atop of each other, as if time itself was tidy little units placed upon end like building blocks or Legos. We're so accustomed to this mental, linear approach to time that most of us probably don't even think twice about it, but the typical notion of chronology is mostly a constructed one: a sun-based calendar from a couple hundred years ago that doesn't accurately represent how we move through space and time.

The Gregorian calendar, the Western format in use for the past several centuries, is a refinement to the previous Julian calendar—the initial division of the year into three hundred and sixty-five days by the Catholic Church based upon arithmetic and a solar calendar rather than the ancient lunar one. Adopted gradually throughout much of the world, it has become our standard notion of time's progression.

Yet our dated, heliocentric model of the solar system has overlooked a hugely important fact: the sun is *not* stationary it is traveling at roughly 45,000 miles (72,420 km) an hour. This means that planets don't simply rotate around it but rather *spiral*—dragged by the sun's gravity as it barrels onward—creating a helix-like vortex in space.

We are spiraling and moving. Always. It feels that we're standing still but Earth spins at 18.5 miles per second, even as we hurtle forward on our spiral (not truly elliptical) trajectory through the galaxy at 155 miles per second. (The seemingly straight path of a falling object, if it falls for one second, has actually traced a spiral at least a hundred and fifty-five miles long.)

Why is this important? Because life happens in a vortex. Everything. From our cellular DNA-helix to the way plants unfurl and grow, life is a spiral—*never* a linear progression. Sometimes it may seem that we are actually traveling backwards or regressing, yet if we visualize our journey (and/or time) as helical, we see that we are simply traversing the curve as it arcs round while still advancing.

Two years ago, I wrote a SAJ post ["Spiraling Through Time: A New Kind of Calendar"] inspired by a spiral labyrinth wall calendar I discovered while living on Maui. The serendipity of the find was perfect, because in writing the final chapter of *The Bones & Breath*, I had just expounded on non-linear thinking, the spiral as blueprint for life, and Earth's spinning trajectory through space—all to underscore that straight lines do not exist in nature or the cosmos, that everything is spiral and arc. *Everything.*

So it was with no small delight that I discovered the Spiral Labyrinth Calendar: the first visual representation of how I actually perceive time—not as a linear construct of twelve months divided into rows of seven days and ending with an odd number, but as an ongoing, endless spiral—mirroring our own progress through the universe. And when we view time as cochlear, we can begin to detect patterns.

Spiraling forward is how I think of any new year. Yes, it offers an opportune moment to mentally/emotionally relinquish the past twelve months that we compartmentalize and conceptualize as a unit. And yet, as with all personal growth and healing, change is never so easy as merely saying goodbye and good riddance—whether it is a pesky behavior, an addiction, or habitual response that no longer serves our highest good. There is a truth in therapy and soul-based transformational work that we seldom shift our limiting behaviors or truly move on from challenging situations until *we also understand how they have aided us in some way.*

There is no magic wand. Not even at New Year. (Consider how often we actually keep those resolutions.)

So as I sat quietly on New Year's Eve, reflecting and writing, thinking back over the events, gifts, challenges, and heartaches of 2015, I considered the strange grace of all those difficulties, shadows, and turbulent stretches of my year's passage. And though I engage it as an ongoing practice, I mused once again how each difficulty taught me something, benefitted me in a curious fashion, or helped to propel me further along the journey. Even in the dark, looking for something to hold onto or believe in.

Life is a conversation waiting for us to show up and engage, to contribute and participate in a meaningful way, to offer something authentic from the soul in return. Each of us has a unique gift to bring. How do we say yes to that creative energy seeking to emerge *through* us? Can we welcome it knowing that we are changed in the process of its emergence, either in the actual choice to dilate past our habitual patterns of restriction, or in the revelation and new understanding that comes through its expression? Or even when its birth feels difficult or painful.

For ages, spirals and labyrinths have been associated with the personal journey or spiritual quest. As the Native Americans and other wisdom-based cultures have long understood, in our own way, each of us travels the Sacred Hoop, progressing through life's stages until returning to the earth. Soul Artists recognize and embrace that life is seasonal and cyclical, that the microcosm mirrors the macrocosm (and vice versa). Life, and time, is not really linear.

Friend, if we open our senses and begin to pay attention to nature, we observe that *everything* is a spiral or arc; it cannot be otherwise on a planet that revolves on its axis while following a rotating, elliptical journey through the cosmos. And although our life journey is not circular, returning us to an exact point, repeatedly we will notice that we have passed this way before—whether in a season now past, or perhaps in a passage or lesson again reappearing for us.

Blessings abound, even amid our difficulties and shadows. As we spin forward into another Gregorian new year, consider apprenticing to wonder and beauty, for they are the magic of everyday life. Too, may each of us dwell in possibility, expansion, and the presence of mysterious grace.

Yes, always *grace*, I say, spiraling back to meet us again and again.

ẹ ẹ ẹ

Mysterious Gifts: Healing and Forgiveness
(January, 2016)

At the rocky shoreline in the late morning, I sat with bare feet in the chilled, gravely sand. Sheltered in the lee of a grey stone monolith, protected from the steady winter wind, I wrapped the charcoal ribbon of cashmere around my neck a bit more snugly.

I have been feeling poorly, struggling with my electromagnetic hypersensitivity (EHS) that makes me weak. So I went to the seashore, for it is always nature—a direct, barefoot connection with earth—that restores and grounds me. Literally. And the further I am from WiFi, so-called "smart meters" and cell phone towers, the better. It is difficult enough to be a highly sensitive person in the modern world, let along the rising tide of electrosmog.

Enfolded by the rumbling voice of the waves—a healing frequency and resonance in its own right—I gazed out at a steely blue sea and watched the gulls as they navigated the wind, calling to each other with mimicking voices. Thirty feet offshore, a couple of California sea otters floated on their backs, like small furry logs with flipper feet, occasionally rolling over to dive and disappear momentarily, then resurfacing.

As I silently steeped in the polysensory coastal experience, breathing deeply into my belly and wriggling my feet down a bit further into the damp grains and stones while focusing on that sensation, I found myself thinking about *healing* and my ongoing connection with it.

I seldom write about the topic, but bodywork and the healing arts have been my profession, on and off, for more than two decades.

I keep thinking that I'm going to retire permanently from this line of work—laying on of hands—but I continue circling back to it. Partly this is because that, despite my love of beautiful food and cooking, the healing arts are far more nourishing and less stressful to me in terms of a day job. Other than brief moments of insanity (which thankfully pass), I have no desire to put on my chef's jacket or apron again to prepare dinner professionally. No, thank you. And much as I would love to simply *write,* wordsmithing doesn't pay enough to live on, at least not at this stretch of my journey.

So, I continue to see clients, and quite often I am surprised and moved by the unexpected healing that unfolds in these sessions. Years ago I developed a curious conviction that whomever arrives for a session is *meant* to have found me—though sometimes the reason may not become clear for either one of us until later.

The other day, I welcomed a new client. Chatting a bit beforehand, I asked him an open-ended query about why he had come to me. He answered that it was because of a testimonial on my bodywork website, particularly the words of a former client who said I was really a shaman. The tall, thin man who sat across from me on the couch was clearly on a quest for some deep healing; he faces an important crossroads in life, wrestling with a grave illness, and is soul searching.

Working with him, as so often happens when my hands switch on and *listen,* words and images began to arrive, messages meant to be shared with the client. I think of them as directives from the firmament. Sometimes they make sense to me, other times not. It isn't my job to judge, interpret or translate, I'm simply the conduit. Like the energy that pours through my palms in sessions, the communication arrives from *beyond*—some nameless place where the soul of healing resides.

With this particular man, a single word rose up in my mind, hovering loudly and refusing to be silenced or disappear until I uttered it aloud. *Forgiveness.* When I spoke it, a wave suddenly rose up and washed through his angular body, wracking him with emotion as he began to weep from a place deep inside. The gates to healing had opened, and involuntarily I drew a full breath in solidarity. My hands continued to work and listen, and there were subsequent messages that I delivered, but somehow this first directive seemed the most powerfully salient.

Forgiveness bridges all of humanity.

Seated at the shoreline, sheltered from the buffeting cold wind by the great jagged stone, I found myself reflecting on forgiving, and how essential it is for healing. What is it we need to pardon in life, whether in ourselves or in others? Perhaps we need to forgive life itself for hurting or disappointing us. Or God. Often it seems most difficult to apply such compassion to ourselves: for our actions or inactions, the seeming failures and shortcomings, or strangely even our gifts and success.

Last week I wrote that the little moments so often shared in this column—a cup of good tea, puttering in the kitchen, the anise-like scent of freshly gathered basil, feeding the birds, watching and listening to the staccato rain—are a balm for the ailments of life. I deeply hold that to be true. Yet I also know that healing is a multifaceted and mysterious process, one that invites introspection and the raw vulnerability of looking into the mirror naked, figuratively or literally. And as I wrote in a New Year post, *we seldom evolve or transform a situation until we understand how it has aided us.*

There are many levels and types of healing—physical, mental, emotional, spiritual—and they are all interrelated. Nothing is really separate, after all.

Compassionate, sensitive touch is profoundly restorative. So too is nature. Both reach beyond the physical to affect other levels of our being. Hence why I was sitting outdoors on a chilly day in January, barefoot on the wet sand, watching and listening to the liquid pewter waves. Grounding. Earthing. Opening all my senses.

I believe that food can be healing and that plants, in particular, are powerful medicine. The transforming power of what we ingest can truly create health—especially when it has been raised with integrity and respect, when good fare honors the earth it came from and the hands that gathered and prepared it. When our sustenance has been acknowledged with gratitude for the gift of its life, whether a chicken or a carrot, when it has been cooked with love, the bodysoul itself is nourished.

Everything is connected.

In our quest for healing, on whatever level, we all need to embrace forgiveness. I write this for my own reminding as surely as for anyone else; for much as I might focus on nourishing the soul—my deliberately built life of little rituals that comfort and sustain—admittedly I have my own list of pardons to work on. It isn't easy. I've a dozen or so bruised hurts and lingering disappointments that it is time to relinquish, yet I keep lugging them around like precious river stones, each one buried in my body somewhere, weighing me down and rounding my shoulders forward.

I wonder, if I carefully unearthed each one, cradling it gently in my hands and then laying it in the winter sun with a soft *thank you* of gratitude and walked away, what lightness might I feel? And what could I plant in those waiting, welcoming spaces instead? Fragrant lavender and unrestrained laughter, perhaps.

Healer, heal thyself.

When we acknowledge the heart and soul, *when we listen and tend our essence,* transformation unfurls like a lotus blossom. Sometimes I think that part of the reason I'm still connected to my healing work with individuals is because each one unknowingly brings me a gift. The messages that come through are powerful reminders for my own growth and guideposts along the path. Clients believe I am helping them, but more likely it is the other way around. Really, *everyone* we meet in life is a teacher (non-humans included, from microbes to mountain lions)— especially the challenging ones.

I wonder, gentle reader, what needs forgiveness in your personal cosmos? And are you willing to embrace it?

Here at the edge of the world, where earth meets sea and sky, perhaps today I can place one foot closer to forgiveness—of self, others, and life—and thus step nearer to my own healing. That would be grace, indeed, for stones are heavy, and best left on a riverbank or seashore where they sing to each other in the moonlight.

Holy, holy...

❧ ❧ ❧

◦*About the* ◦*Author*

L.R. Heartsong is a healer who writes, teaching a sensual connection with life, nature, and the Soul of the World.

A body-centered therapist trained in somatic psychology, he became a Paris-trained chef (briefly a cook for the rich and famous), until his intuition and heart led him back to the healing arts, along with nature-based soul work.

Living in England, a revelation while crossing a Kentish field at twilight propelled him to write *The Bones & Breath: A Man's Guide to Eros, the Sacred Masculine, and the Wild Soul.* Upon returning to America, as part of his quest to get the book published, he launched the Soul Artist Journal, which slowly grew in popularity.

After nearly five years of weekly posts, Heartsong closed the cover on the Journal and began TendingSacred: lengthier, monthly writing along a healer's path (2017–2019). At the outset of 2020, he returned to the kitchen with a pen and camera in hand for a new offering: **Sage, Salt & Fire**—exploring the Art of Nourishing Body and Soul. Through recipes, his writings, and an online course, River illuminates how to create a beautiful, healing relationship with food... and life.

Heartsong has been a featured presenter in multiple podcasts, as well as global online symposiums featuring change-making influencers (scientists, shamans, mystics, psychologists, healers, and more). He hosts the Embodied Soul Podcast, and works with clients internationally through his signature 10-week Evolutionary BodySoul program—fusing vibrant health and soul.

Learn more at **soulquests.com** & **sagesaltandfire.com**

Acknowledgments

During the years of writing the weekly Soul Artist Journal, from many sources I constantly drew inspiration, perspective, strength, and the willingness to continue with my giveaway. As with the previous volume, a few special mentions are in order.

ఴ

Gaia, the Wild Beloved. We tend to use the word "nature" as if it were something out there, separate from ourselves when, in fact, right down to our microbes, we are indivisible and inseparable from the *suprasomatic sentience* in which we are constantly steeped. Yet I remain deeply indebted to the wild shorelines, verdant fields, whispering woods, and dry arroyos where I have walked and sought solace, inspiration, and healing. Endless blessings to the dear, beautiful trees.

All the readers of the Journal. As stated in the Preface, it was you that so-often kept me going—especially when I felt reluctant (unable, even) to deliver another Sunday offering. Bless you for reading, sharing, and the lovely comments via email and social media. It was my great privilege to offer you these glimpses of beauty, magic, wonder, and mysterious grace as nourishment for the soul.

Sara, the Good Witch of Kent. Steadfast reader, confidant, and super-spooky friend. I surely would not have made it through all the shadows and pitfalls without your friendship, emails, and generous parcels of goodies. I've said it before: you remain the very best that England has to offer. Please do come round for tea tomorrow.

ZuVuYah, "sparkle fairy" *extraordinaire*. Bless you for combing through these selections as an advance reader, employing your Venus in Virgo attention to detail, catching my typos. This is a better book because of your time and diligence, and I am so very glad to have you in my orbit. Here's to another trip round the sun, sister.

Robert, *mon petit*. As always, there are no adequate words, love. Bless you for everything, every day. I go on choosing you, and we go onwards together, searching for home but always creating it in our hearts, wherever the painted gypsy caravan may be parked; a couple of flickering candles on the table, something delicious on our plates, and two lazy English Whippets underfoot. *Je t'aime... toujours.*